THE MASTER ARCHITECT SERIES II

MITCHELL/GIURGOLA ARCHITECTS

Selected and Current Works

THE MASTER ARCHITECT SERIES II

MITCHELL/GIURGOLA ARCHITECTS

Selected and Current Works

Meeting Places

Work Places

Research/Study Places

Public Spaces/Places

First published in Australia in 1996 by
The Images Publishing Group Pty Ltd
ACN 059 734 431
6 Bastow Place, Mulgrave, Victoria, 3170
Telephone (61 3) 9561 5544 Facsimile (61 3) 9561 4860

National Library of Australia Cataloguing-in-Publication Data

Mitchell/Giurgola Architects.
Mitchell/Giurgola Architects: selected and current works.

Bibliography.
Includes index.
ISBN 1 875498 50 8.
Master Architect Series II ISSN 1320 7253

1. Mitchell/Giurgola Architects. 2. Architecture, American.
3. Architecture, Modern—20th century—United States.
4. Architects—United States. I. Title. II.
Architects. (Series: Master Architect Series II).

720.973

Edited by Stephen Dobney

Designed by Laurent Marrier d'Unienville for Blur Pty Ltd, Mulgrave, Australia

Film separations by Scanagraphix Australia Pty Ltd

Printing by Everbest Printing, Hong Kong

This book is dedicated to Ehrman B. Mitchell and Romaldo Giurgola, founders of the firm, who have provided great inspiration and support to the current generation of partners.

Contents

8 Introduction
The Aesthetic Dimension
By Mildred F. Schmertz, FAIA

Selected and Current Works 1986–1996

Meeting Places

18 Anchorage Historical and Fine Arts Museum
30 Advanced Business Institute, IBM Corporation
44 Virginia Air and Space Center/Hampton Roads History Center
54 Fine and Performing Arts Center, University of West Florida
60 Onondaga County Convention Center
72 Harlem International Trade Center

Research/Study Places

78 George M. Low Center for Industrial Innovation, Rensselaer Polytechnic Institute
86 Outpatient Care Center, University of California at Los Angeles
92 Revelle College Sciences Building, University of California at San Diego
98 Life Sciences Building, Ciba Pharmaceuticals
108 Ceramics Corridor Innovation Center, Corning
112 Ceramics Corridor Innovation Center, Alfred
116 Stafford Hall, Microbiology/Orthopaedics Research Building, University of Vermont
124 Laboratory Science Building, College of Staten Island
128 Metcalfe Student Center, Long Island University
130 Zeckendorf Health Sciences Center, Long Island University
136 Administrative and Student Services Building, Hostos Community College
138 PS 88, The Seneca School
140 PS 56, Richmond Elementary School

Work Places

146 Volvo Corporate Headquarters

160 300 Atlantic Street Office Building

166 Center West, Office/Retail/Parking

174 Solana Office/Parking Complex,
IBM Corporation/Maguire Partners

186 Columbus Center

196 The Lighthouse Inc. Headquarters

Public Spaces/Places

210 Hudson View East Residential Development

214 Davenport Downtown Plan and River Center Plaza

216 Intertech Corporation, Office Development Master Plan

218 St Joseph's College Comprehensive Plan

220 Southampton College Master Plan

222 The Belvedere, Battery Park City

Firm Profile

233 Biographies

238 Collaborating Partners

241 Chronological List of Selected Buildings & Projects

247 Selected Design Awards

249 Bibliography

252 Acknowledgments

255 Index

The Aesthetic Dimension

By Mildred F. Schmertz, FAIA

In the United States, small to medium-sized architectural firms founded by acknowledged design masters rarely give birth to a successful second generation. Only large, corporate firms last long enough to celebrate 50 and 100 year anniversaries. Outstanding among the few exceptions to this rule is the 37-year-old firm of Mitchell/Giurgola Architects, now headed by five partners who began work at the New York City office in the late 60s and early 70s. Paul Broches, Steven M. Goldberg, Jan Keane, John M. Kurtz, and Mark J. Markiewicz practice an architecture of the highest distinction, as heads of a 35-person office that has grown significantly over the last 10 years, both in its volume and range of work. Founding partner Romaldo Giurgola lives and works in Canberra, Australia as a partner of Mitchell/Giurgola & Thorp Architects, while co-founder Ehrman B. Mitchell Jr retired in 1984. All of the present partners except Markiewicz, who studied architecture at Princeton, were students of Giurgola's at the universities of Pennsylvania or Columbia. Each was invited by Giurgola to join the firm soon after graduation, and has remained to work there ever since.

Volvo Corporate Headquarters

In the pages that follow, 31 works are illustrated, all completed or initiated in the past decade. The collection includes a wide range of building types: office buildings, museums and exhibition halls, schools and colleges, research laboratories and health service facilities, and renovations. By contrast, most US architectural firms of comparable size and talent tend to specialize. The architects bring the same rigorous professional focus to additions to existing low-profile buildings governed by severe budget constraints as they do to high-profile public, cultural, or commercial buildings.

In all their projects, the Mitchell/Giurgola partners focus upon program development, generating building designs that are both responsive and faithful to the client's needs. At the same time, if appropriate, their design strategies transcend the client's original intentions, assisting users to expect and obtain more from the program than they might have originally anticipated. Basing their designs on intensive program analysis has earned the firm clients with very complex functional requirements, often related to applications of high technology. The architects' analytical methodology helps create a unique character for each project. Just as importantly, however, a project will possess its own aesthetic dimension, governed by formal themes that, from the beginning, have guided the practice.

In all their work, the architects hope to achieve a quality they call "resonance," defined as a visual or conceptual linkage with buildings or places they most admire. While for them such models of mastery may include relatively new arrivals on the contemporary scene, most of their architecture connects to classical Modernist sources, notably the work of Gunnar Asplund, Alvar Aalto, and Louis I. Kahn. The partners use this tradition as a source of form, where it suits the logic of a particular program. Occasionally, older historic influences appear. For example, in developing the parti of the Anchorage Historical and Fine Arts Museum in Anchorage, Alaska (1984), a major addition to an existing museum, they have employed a device as old as the temples of Egypt and as close to the present as the work of Kahn—that of signifying a special place by setting its building within an outer building, consisting of screen-like layers of wall. On the south facade is a procession of four serrated brick walls 45 feet high. The first fully encloses its projecting space; the second is half vertical enclosure, half two-story colonnade; the third and fourth are each punctuated by five-bay arcades below enclosed second-story space, with two-story colonnades at the corners. Their rhythmic cadence echoes the more monumental stepped-back facade of a federal office building across the street. A free-standing tower defines the opposite corner. On the east facade is a miniature colonnade screening a children's gallery and terrace. These extra layers of wall on the east and south facades endow the institution with a civic and cultural presence that could not have been achieved by a tight boundary at the sidewalk edge.

The manner in which boundaries are defined is but one consideration, however significant, within a controlling compositional idea that governs all the firm's design. The architects perceive each building as an assembly of fragments within its environment: episodes along a route of axes and paths

Anchorage Historical and Fine Arts Museum

Anchorage Historical and Fine Arts Museum

that, taken together, form a clear and powerful synthesis of architectonic mass and shape, building systems, art and craft, topography, and landscape—in harmonious relationship with the space it inhabits. The force driving this synthesis is the architects' primary intention to give form and clarity to the functional and social significance of the building program, while serving to the highest degree possible human pleasures and needs.

Advanced Business Institute

The IBM Corporation Advanced Business Institute in Palisades, New York (1989) is a brilliant realization of this conception. Offering corporate-level business training to invited groups of executive customers, IBM required a building that bespoke its status as an institution, and its regard for the business stature of its students. Within the IBM complex, architecture is experienced aesthetically as a series of important points along an itinerary. In its landscape, two major axes at right angles focus upon, clarify, and connect the three major functions of the complex—reception, education, and housing. This classical geometric order is interwoven with informal paths that invite the visitor to meander through a gently rolling landscape of meadow, lake, and woods. The north–south axis spans and intersects the entire three-to-five-story brick complex, extending northward across the pond to the woodland housing, and southward to the classroom wing. Bisected by the north– south axis and centered on the east–west driveway axis is a classically symmetrical entrance pavilion, the focus of the composition. This elegant fragment displays by its form and richness the high corporate purpose of the entire facility. The first signal of such distinction is the handsome curvilinear glass and steel entrance canopy, supported by steel columns encased in teak. A well-conceived, elliptical, oculus-lit reception area is the next point on the itinerary, itself but an introduction to the most powerful symbolic space of the complex—the three-story main lounge, designed as the institute's principal setting for communal gathering. Square in plan, warmed by an immense open fireplace and lit by clerestory windows that follow the profile of its roof trusses, the room is completely glazed on its west facade to offer a fine view of the pond. Throughout the complex, all communal spaces inhabited by IBM's executive guests share elegance of form, scale, materials, and craftsmanship. Noteworthy are the pond-oriented dining room, lit by a great curvilinear skylight, and five "coffee-break pavilions" adjoining a classroom corridor to encourage informal meetings between classes.

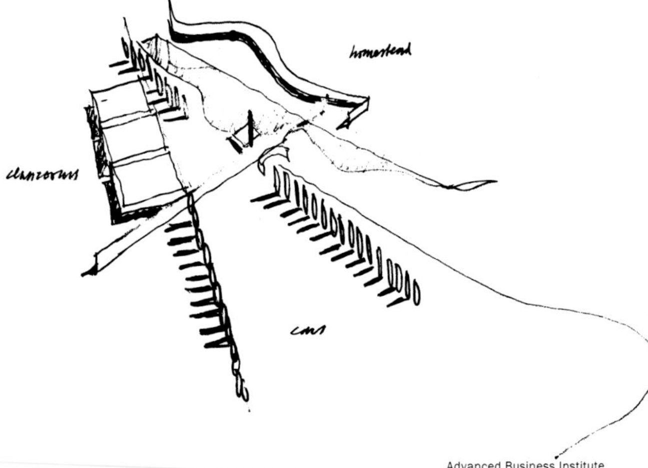

Advanced Business Institute

For all its qualities, the architects are not likely to produce another corporate conference center that closely resembles this complex for IBM. To do so would be counter to their belief that because functional and social significance can differ from one building type to another, and even within building types, so should the architecture these forces engender. The Life Sciences Building for the Ciba Pharmaceuticals Division in Summit, New Jersey (1993–1995) makes this point. What this research laboratory has in common with other buildings by the firm is the analytical approach by which the program and solution were developed. The completed building itself is one of a kind.

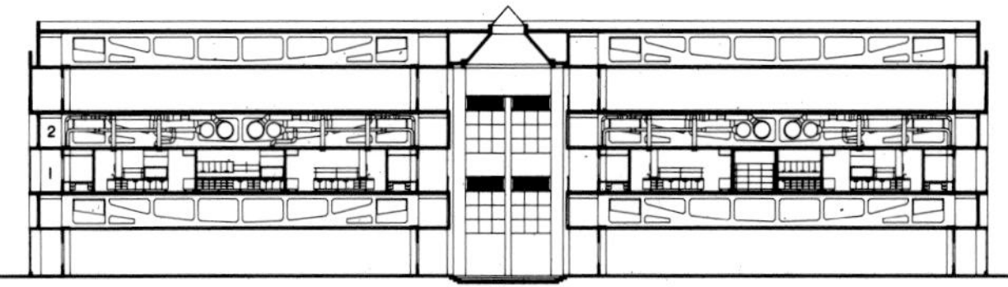

Life Sciences Building

As for most laboratories, the program required adaptability to short- and long-term change, and energy efficiency. The laboratory, while technologically complex in its mechanical systems, electrical components, and other services, is shaped by a direct and simple modular plan and section. Immense, by laboratory standards, it comprises 440,000 square feet, divided into three interconnected three-story blocks that tightly fill its site within the Ciba campus. Loft-like laboratory spaces allow a variety of plan configurations. The laboratories in the central block have direct access to the three-story animal space, while those in the east and west blocks overlook three-story skylit atriums, bisected by formal water courses. Supporting lab floors and roof are rows of open-web trusses, that form interstitial space through which laboratory services are threaded.

Because the laboratory scientists are engaged in intellectually demanding activities, yet are confined by their tasks to small offices and equipment-packed labs, the architects made these spaces feel as open as possible, and brought maximum natural light into them. Furthermore they provided throughout the building serene, pleasant, day-lit communal spaces for relaxation and the exchange of ideas. The building's itinerary is a compact yet fluid one. All principal corridors connect with the atria and follow the perimeters of the laboratory blocks. These passageways overlook a well planted landscape and receive ample natural light by means of generous fenestration filling each modular bay.

Life Sciences Building

The conception of architecture as itinerary is based upon a visual aesthetic, derived from the appearance and sequence of building fragments and landscape as one moves by. For the Lighthouse Inc. in New York City (1995), an organization that teaches the visually impaired to function independently in mainstream society, the architects devised a series of spaces and pathways for a community of people with partial or no vision within a bright and spirited environment for the sighted who work at and visit the center. The firm focused sharply on every imaginable spatial encounter a person under the institution's care would ever have along the dark paths of his handicap. The program was not without constraints, as it required the total rehabilitation of the institution's existing quarters—a 14-story office tower completed in 1964 on a dense midtown Manhattan site. More space was created by the addition of an extra floor at the base and top, and a new building to the north. The interiors were completely reconfigured. Within this typical office tower envelope, the architects skillfully managed to assemble, interconnect, and make legible, accessible, and comfortable to all users, a set of widely differing functions including a street-level store; a performing arts and conference center; a child development center; a low-vision clinic; computer technology and employment training facilities; a music school and library; vision and research labs; and administrative and office space. A visually impaired person, finding his way through this complex facility, is guided by tactile and visual clues and maps, devised by the architects to assure his confidence and safety. Upon touching notched railings he expects changes in level; feeling tactile or observing color contrast warning strips in the floor he locates the main staircase; perceiving high color and tonal contrast at door and elevator door frames and at intersections of wall base and floor, he orients himself and avoids collisions. To the sighted, the building is a handsome, pleasant facility; for people with vision impairment it must be the most accommodating and responsive place they know.

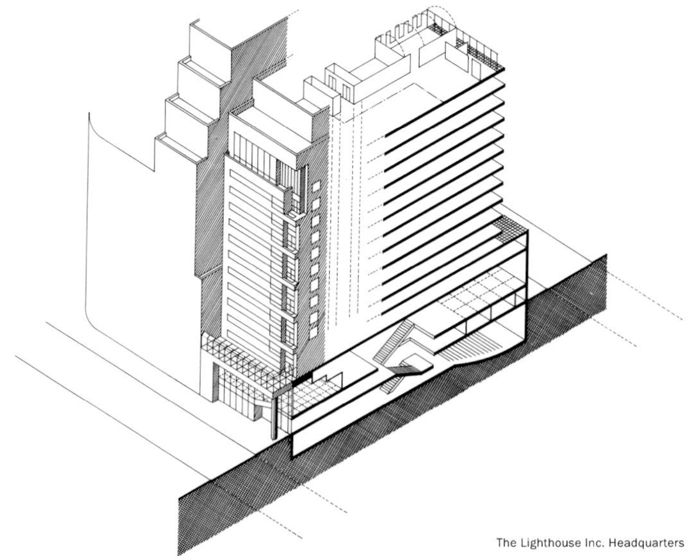

The Lighthouse Inc. Headquarters

Parks are obvious itineraries, and their aesthetic dimension is not a mysterious attribute. They are either beautiful and happy places to be, or they aren't, and the ordinary user has no trouble perceiving the difference. Now complete in New York City is the 1.6-acre Belvedere (1995), the newest segment of the nearly completed 1.5-

The Lighthouse Inc. Headquarters

mile-long continuous linear waterfront park that follows the Hudson River from Chambers Street all the way to Battery Park at the southernmost tip of Manhattan. As a landscape design, the Belvedere is less functionally and technologically complex than much of Mitchell/Giurgola's architecture. As a result, the formal themes it shares with the four other projects discussed in this essay are perhaps more readily perceived. Designed in collaboration with landscape architect Susan Child, and situated within the sector dominated by the three skyscrapers of the World Financial Center, this beautiful urban park is at the very core of the mixed-use development. To the south, clusters of high-rise luxury housing are bordered by a well conceived and planted esplanade. To the north, a residential neighborhood, as yet unbuilt, already has its ideal setting—a popular family park edged by playgrounds and pavilions at the boundary of an elongated, informal, meandering lawn. The southern edge of the Belvedere borders the dockside of a small, lively, yacht-filled harbor. To the east it directly abuts the hard-edged, multi-stepped plaza that fronts the skyscrapers. At its center, at the river edge, is the Trans-Hudson Ferry Terminal. The Belvedere is a fragment of the itineraries of several types of users—walkers, rollerbladers, and cyclists who may be traversing the entire waterfront park, New Jersey commuters by the thousands who make their way back and forth between the ferry terminal and their offices in lower Manhattan, and those who simply want to sit and relax in leafy shade.

Since the Belvedere connects two styles of landscape—the free-form, grassy park to the north, and the angular geometries of the corporate plaza to the east—the architects created a park which is both informal and formal. To do so, they carefully avoided continuing the more obvious patterns and characteristics of the adjacent spaces, nor did they attempt the dramatic or spectacular. The curvilinear contours of the residential park are subtly echoed in the serpentine shape of the Belvedere's battered wall of beautifully detailed and constructed rusticated Dakota granite (suggested by the fortifications at the base of the nearby Statue of Liberty). This wall separates the lower river esplanade from a broad elevated terrace area gridded with a bosque of English oaks that both softens and eases the transition between it and the corporate

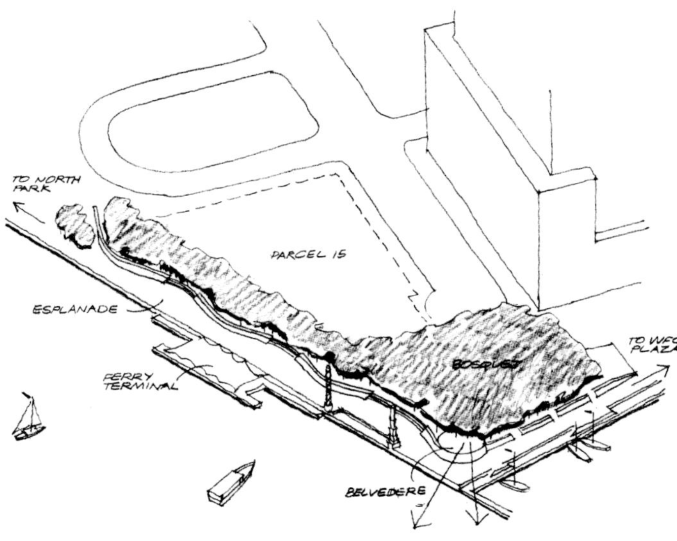

The Belvedere, Battery Park City

The Belvedere, Battery Park City

The Belvedere, Battery Park City

The Belvedere, Battery Park City

plaza. The terrace connects to the north with an allee of oaks. The upper and lower levels are joined at intervals by staircases intersecting the wall, the most monumental of these leading from the river esplanade to the terrace bosque. The serpentine form culminates at the south corner in a circular belvedere planted in honey locusts, overlooking New York Harbor and the Statue of Liberty.

Given the Belvedere's civic and recreational importance, the architects decided the park should have a distinctive monument, to mark its presence and welcome those entering Battery Park City by yacht or ferry. The sculptor Martin Puryear was chosen to design the monument, and created two immense stainless steel pylons, one an open lattice 73 feet, 5 inches high, and the other a closed form 56 feet, 6 inches high. Intricately imposing works of sculpture by day, and illuminated beacons at night, they are the latest and by far the most successful of the series of installations of public art located within the Battery Park development. Correct in scale and powerful as image, their excellence is fundamentally architectural; an example, among many, of the skill with which the architects collaborate with allied arts and crafts. Another successful instance of such effort is the Volvo Corporation Headquarters in Gothenburg, Sweden, that displays beautifully detailed materials and finishes, as well as murals and other works of art by Lin Utzon and Jennifer Bartlett.

All five projects—the Anchorage museum, the IBM campus, the Ciba research facility, the Lighthouse, and the Belvedere—were chosen because they express with great clarity and distinction the qualities common to all the firm's architecture, whether civic, cultural, corporate, educational, or devoted to health care and research. The master plans of the IBM campus and the Belvedere are splendidly ordered and arranged, yet filled with quiet small-scaled amenity, attributes to be found in all of the firm's site planning. The dignified and imposing presence of the Anchorage museum is characteristic of all the firm's institutional work in urban locations. The programmatic precision, in combination with spatial and structural inventiveness, that distinguishes the Ciba research facility governs all their projects, whatever the building type. Finally, Mitchell/Giurgola's successful effort at the Lighthouse to create an aesthetic to serve and satisfy the needs of the visually impaired and the sighted, displays the interest and zeal the architects always bring to new architectural challenges.

Volvo Corporate Headquarters

MEETING PLACES

Anchorage Historical and Fine Arts Museum

Design/Completion 1982/1984
Anchorage, Alaska
Municipality of Anchorage
Associate architect: Maynard and Partch
27,800 square feet renovation
68,000 square feet addition
47,000 square feet parking
Light and dark beige brick, brownstone trim and red granite panels

The new museum rises in a series of steps, culminating in a monumentally scaled front facade which establishes a coherent relationship between an existing one-story museum to the north and a five-story federal building to the south. The stepped building front creates a dramatic entry from the east and provides views to downtown. Framed views of the Chugach Mountains in the upper gallery areas and a generous sculpture plaza to the south take advantage of the striking Alaskan light.

The east facade is deliberately contrasted with the formal south elevation, the major pedestrian approach to the museum. The children's activity area and gallery, with associated sculpture garden and extensive landscaping, offer an inviting, human scale.

Interior spaces are organized around a large light-filled central courtyard which provides a clear sense of orientation. Visitors experience a processional sequence of public arrival, courtyard tranquility and finally, the serenity of the galleries.

"The courtyard serves as a metaphor for the natural environment through the introduction of water, slate floors, wood walls, and an oculus opening to the sky."
Steven M. Goldberg, FAIA

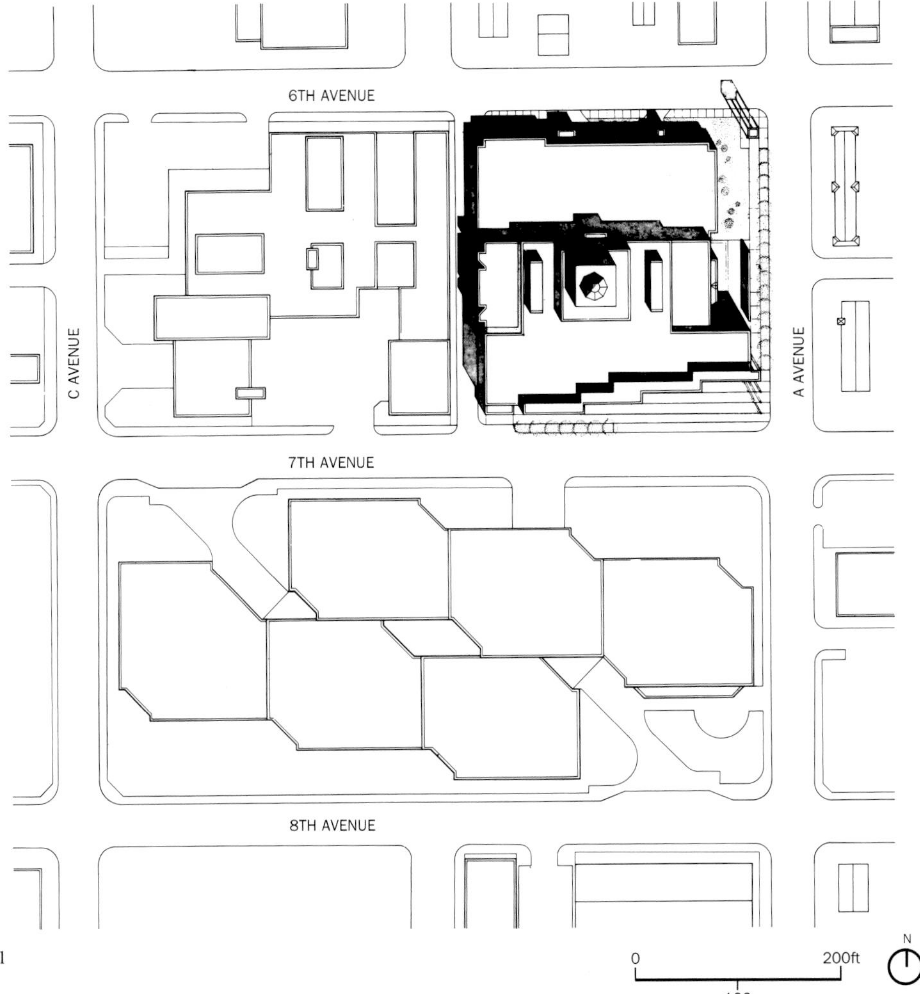

1

2

3

4

1 Site plan
2 View from south-east
3 Entry portico
4 View looking east

5 View of east elevation
6&7 Lighting concept sketches
8 View looking south
9 Entry plaza

5

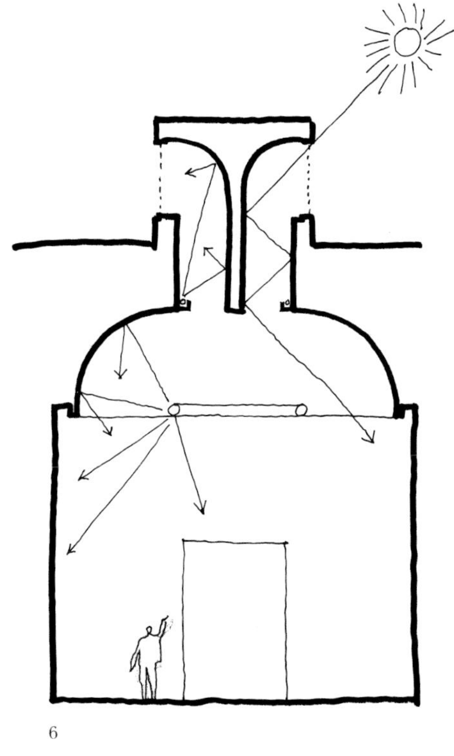

6

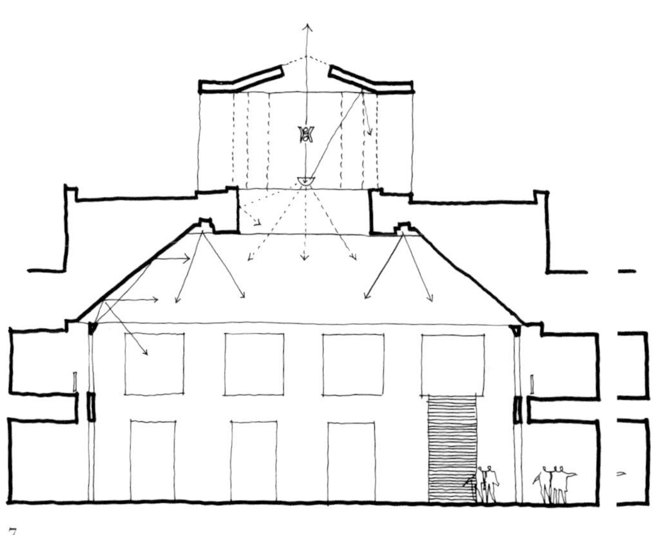

7

8

9

1 Vestibule
2 Lobby
3 Coat room
4 Lecture hall
5 Shop
6 Office
7 Lounge
8 Classroom
9 Courtyard
10 Permanent gallery
11 Temporary gallery
12 Junior gallery
13 Activity area
14 Exhibit preparation/ storage
15 Kitchen
16 Service
17 Parking entry

Existing building

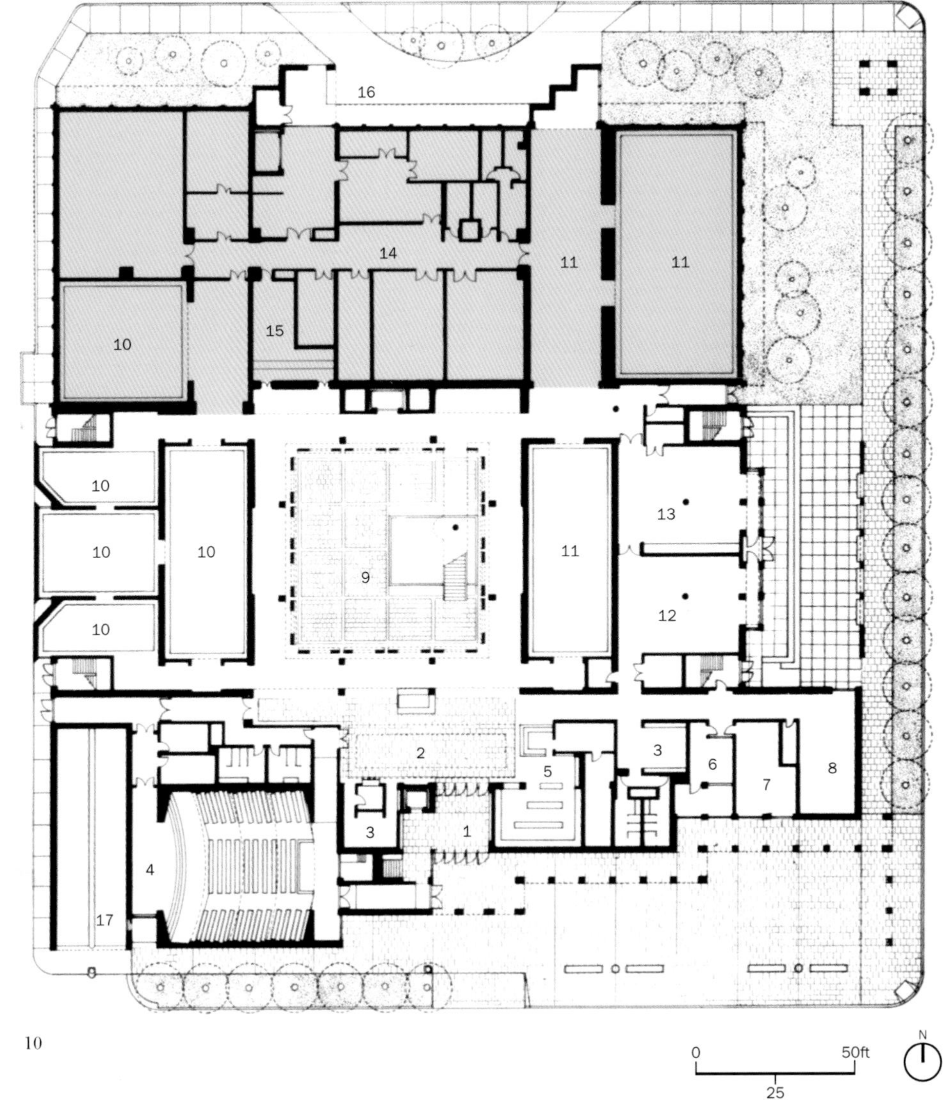

10

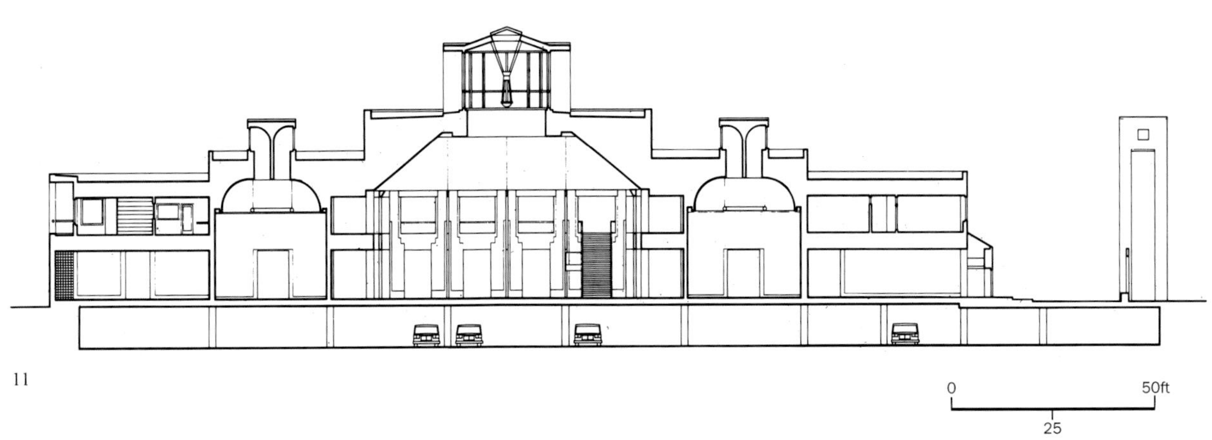

11

10 Ground level plan
11 East–west section
12 Second-floor plan
13 North–south section

1 Open to below
2 Library
3 Administration
4 Native people/
History of Alaska gallery

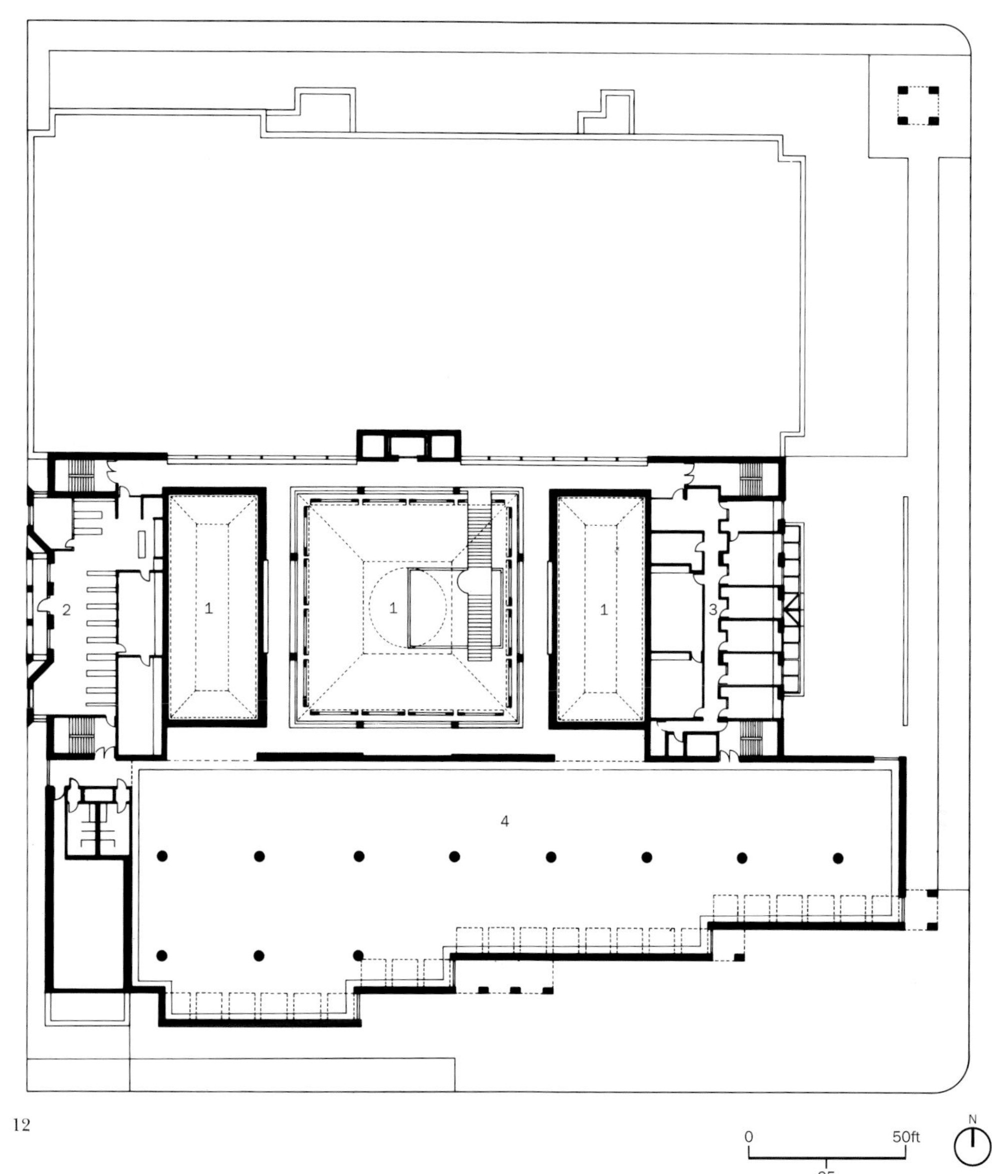

12

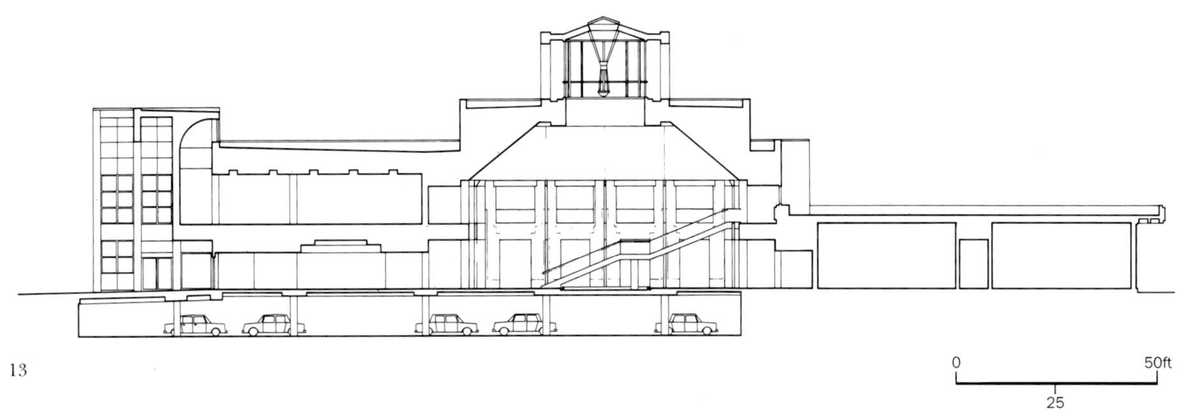

13

14

15

14 Lantern over atrium
15 Main staircase and atrium seen from upper gallery
16 Lobby/reception
17 Grand stair to upper galleries
18 Central atrium

16

17

18

19

20

21

22

19 Atrium seen from upper galleries
20 History of Alaska gallery looking west
21 History of Alaska gallery south wall looking east
22 History of Alaska gallery south wall

23

24

23 Lecture hall
24 Permanent gallery
25 Lecture hall
26 Permanent gallery

25

26

Advanced Business Institute

Design/Completion 1983/1989
Palisades, New York
IBM Corporation
194,850 square feet education
138,560 square feet guest rooms
99,590 square feet dining/recreation
Rose-colored molded brick, teak and mahogany windows and trim, terne-metal roofs, maple cabinetry

The Advanced Business Institute is an executive conference center and retreat for IBM's most important customers, with 200 guest rooms, dining and recreation amenities, and interactive on-line educational and demonstration spaces.

The site is a pastoral, densely wooded, rolling 106 acres. The village-like institute accommodates distinct program components around a series of interconnected ponds. The use of natural building materials sets a warm and intimate backdrop for sophisticated educational technology.

Three major components are connected by bridges and galleries that provide access and views to the ponds. A central element houses the reception/dining functions, a serpentine wing to the north houses the residential rooms and fitness center, and a three-story wing to the south houses the education/administration functions.

"Articulation of the massing, transparency and light, together with natural materials, creates a fluid relationship between the building elements and the surrounding woodland." Paul Broches, FAIA

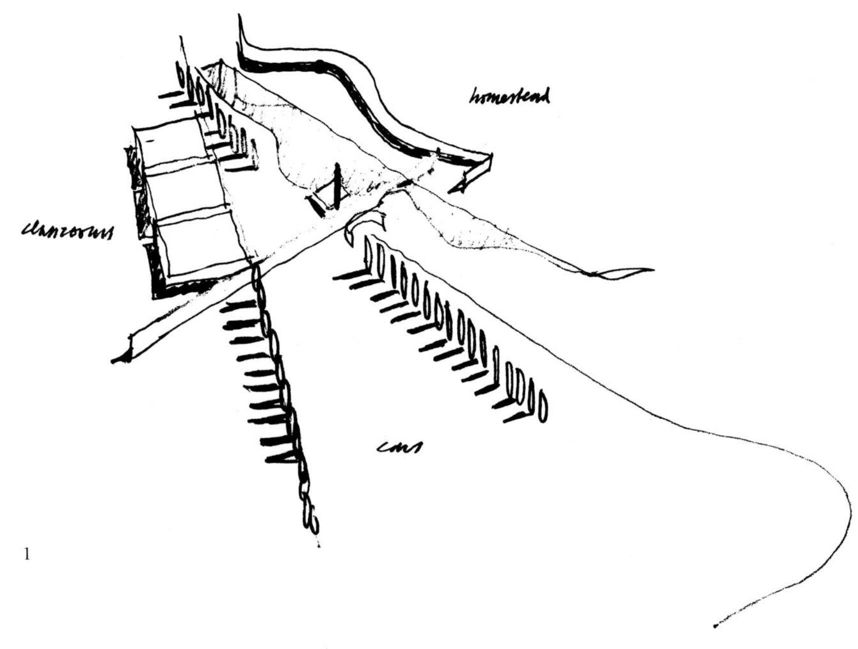

1

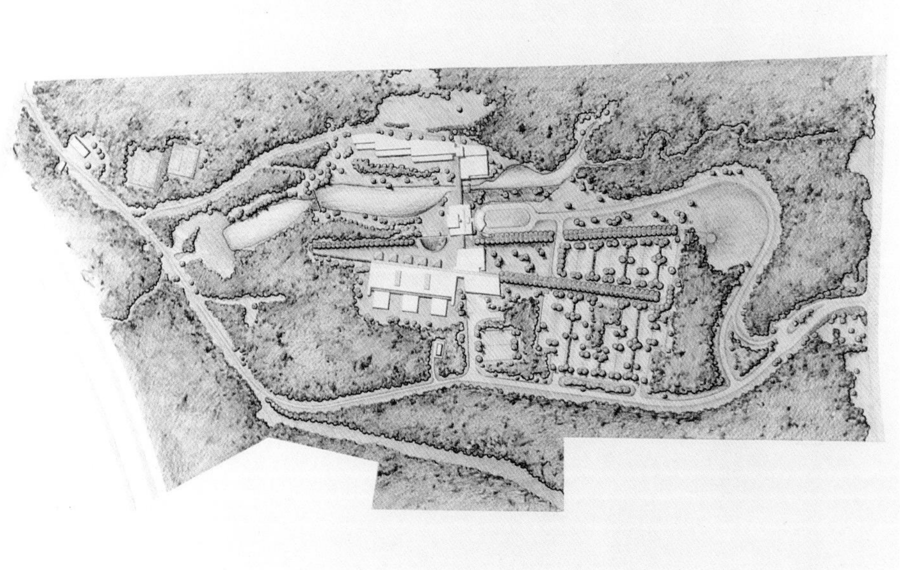

2

3

4

1 Conceptual diagram
2 Illustrated site plan
3 Main entry and drop-off area
4 Pedestrian bridge linking residential and classroom facilities

5

6

7

8

5 Residential wing looking north-east
6 Main lounge seen across central pond
7 Classroom coffee break pavilions with lower dining facilities
8 Section through residential, dining, and classroom wings

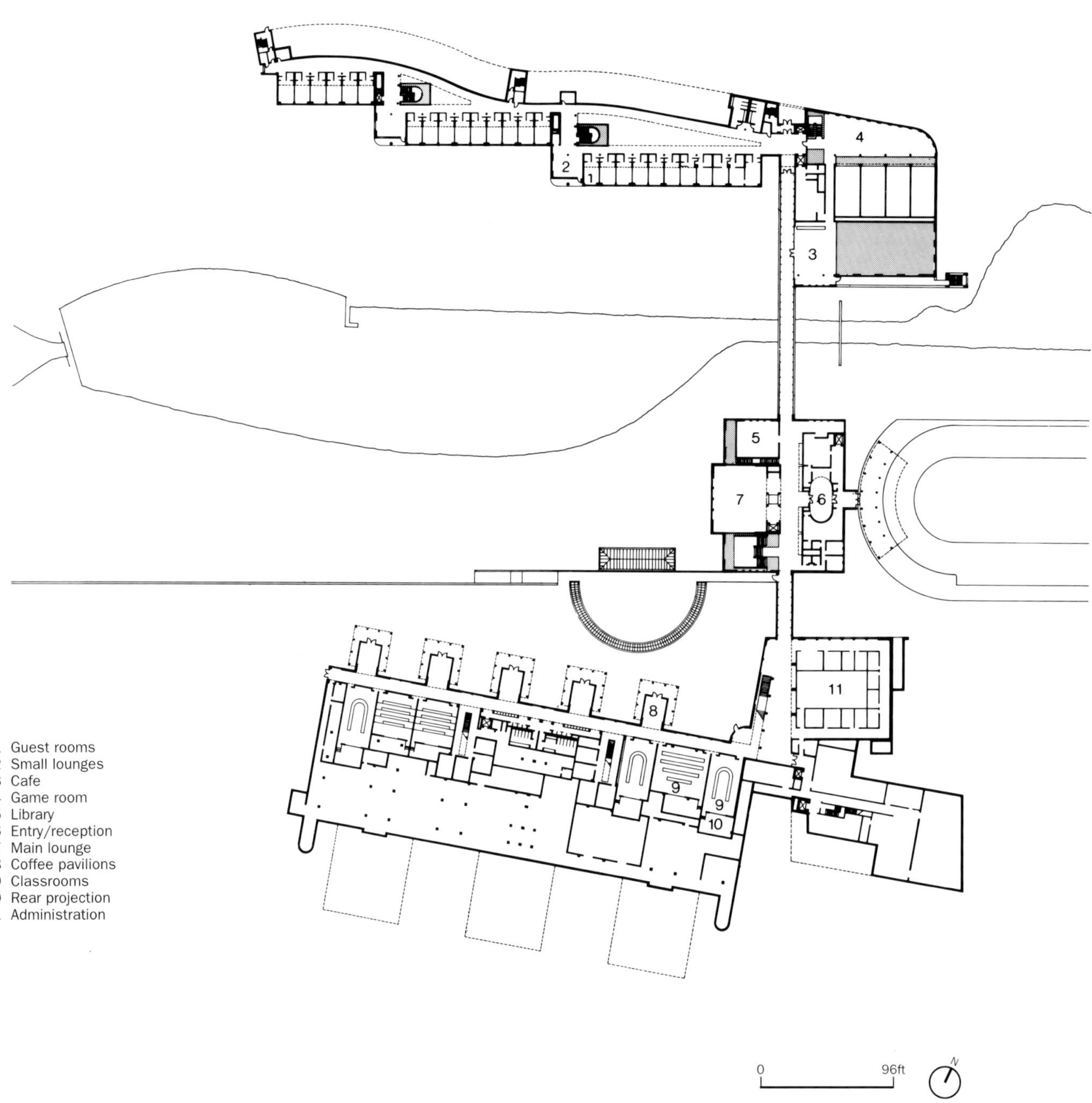
1 Guest rooms
2 Small lounges
3 Cafe
4 Game room
5 Library
6 Entry/reception
7 Main lounge
8 Coffee pavilions
9 Classrooms
10 Rear projection
11 Administration
0 96ft
N

9

10

11

12

9 Entry level plan
10 Main entry canopy
11 Detail of coffee break pavilion
12 Main entry canopy looking north

13

13 Glazed dining terrace
14 The great hall

14

15

15&16 Coffee break pavilion
17 Section through lounge/entry
18 Main dining room

16

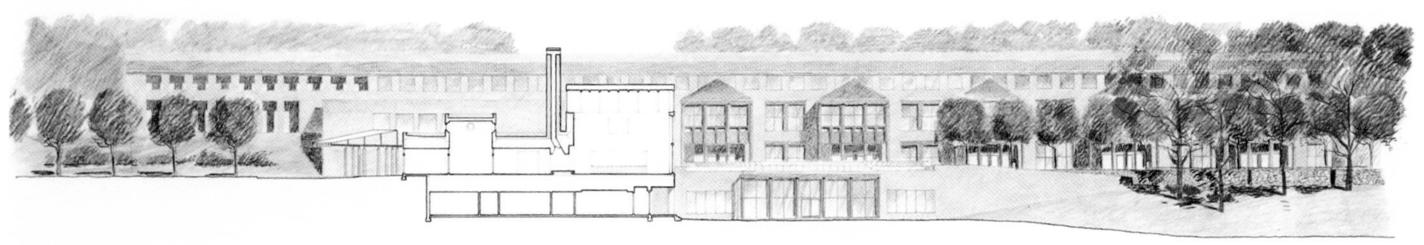

17

18

19

20

21

22

19 Stair to dining rooms
20 Main dining room
21 Residential atrium stair
22 Stair to instructors' offices

23

24

25

23 On-line classroom
24 96-seat classroom
25 Harvard-style classroom
26–28 Guest bedroom

26

27

28

Virginia Air and Space Center/ Hampton Roads History Center

Design/Completion 1987/1992
Hampton, Virginia
Virginia Air and Space Center
Associate architect: Rancorn Wildman Krause Brezinski
118,000 square feet
Concrete piers, metal trusses and roof
Brick, aluminum and glass cladding

Located in the downtown waterfront district, the new Air and Space Center reinforces a strong relationship between the waterfront and the renovated city core. The museum is dedicated to exploration and discovery, depicting the centuries between colonial settlement and space exploration.

Circulation to and within the museum, the large open space in front of the building, and the arcade along the north wall all reinforce existing and proposed pedestrian patterns. The building perimeter is of two-story brick-faced elements compatible with surrounding buildings.

The central space houses large exhibits. Galleries at the periphery and on the second level have smaller-scale displays. The entrance lobby and museum shop are in the most public area of the site, and opposite is a 300-seat IMAX theater. Other spaces include a research library and offices.

"The challenge was to create a building which would be an appropriate symbol of the region's important role in space exploration and to make a connection to Hampton's historic downtown." John Kurtz, AIA

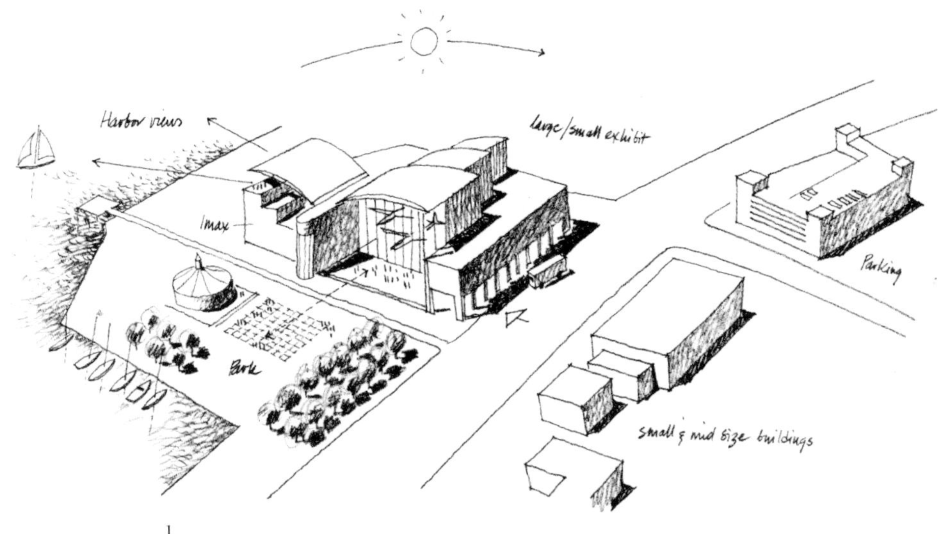

1

2

3

1 Building in context
2 View of west facade
3 Detail view of east facade

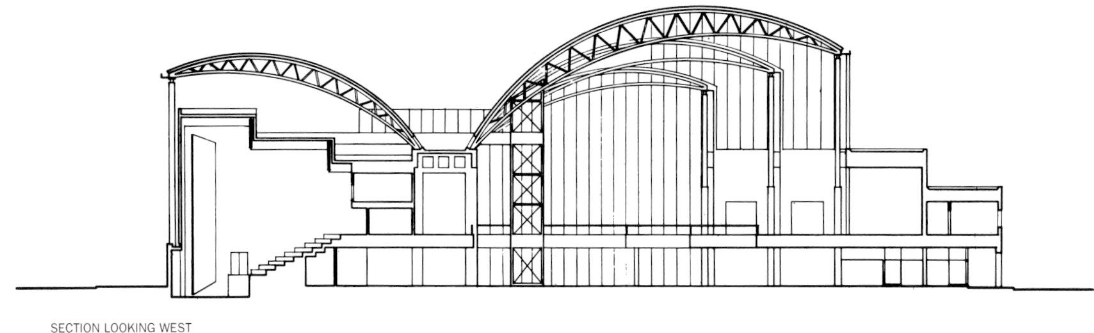

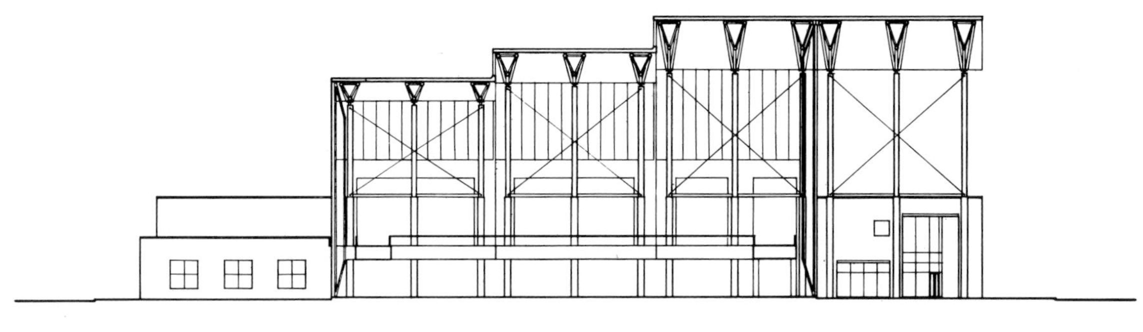

4

5

4 Sections
5 View of south facade from harbor
6 Main entry at north-east corner

6

7 Detail of IMAX Theatre structure
8 Detail of east facade window wall
9 View of east facade from harbor
10 Aerial view looking south-west
11 East facade at night

7

8

9

10

11

12

13

14

0 50ft 25 N

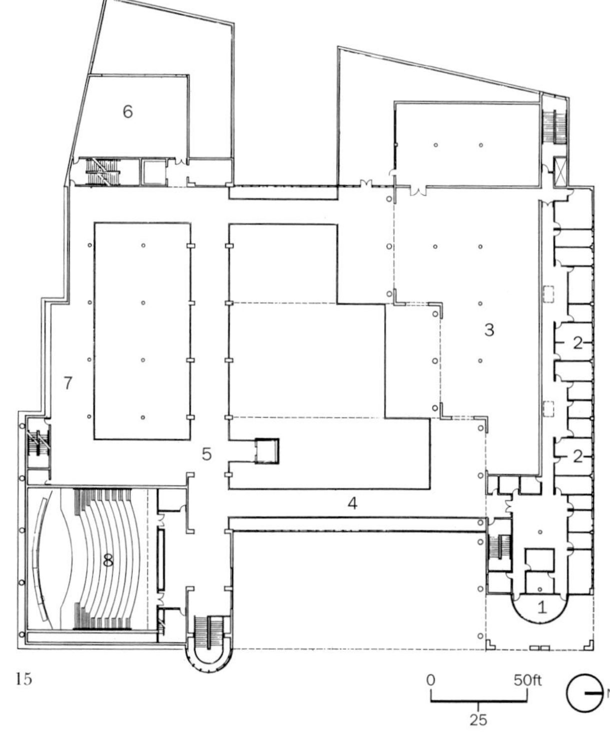

15

1 Lobby
2 Plaza
3 Reception
4 Gift shop
5 Classroom
6 Aviation exhibits
7 History exhibits
8 IMAX theater

1 Library
2 Staff offices
3 Space exhibits
4 Mezzanine
5 Air Force exhibits
6 Mechanical
7 Exhibit mezzanine
8 IMAX theater

12 Bridge at east facade
13 Landings with observation points
14 Ground level plan
15 Second-floor plan
16 View from elevator
17 Interior exhibit space—main level

16

17

18

18 Interior exhibit space—second level
19 Interior exhibit space—gantry level

19

Fine and Performing Arts Center

Design/Completion 1987/1992
Pensacola, Florida
The University of West Florida
Associate Architect: Barrett, Daffin and Carlan, Inc.
87,000 square feet
Masonry, stucco and glass walls, painted metal roofs, aluminum windows, concrete floors and paths

Three departments: music, theater, and art are brought together in a new humanities complex for a major southern university. Each department is composed of academic and performance/exhibition components.

Spaces for the Department of Music include practice rooms, offices, a rehearsal room, and a 300-seat recital hall. A 450-seat modified proscenium theater with stage house and orchestra pit, a 100-seat studio theater, costume and scene shops, dressing rooms, and offices serve the Theater Department. The Art Department includes eleven studios for student instruction, eight faculty offices, and an art gallery.

In both the massing of the building and the plan organization, individual elements are articulated. A series of courtyards and arcades help to define and weave together the different components, as well as enhance the relationship of the building to the natural environment.

"A new square provides a focal point of the 'arts village,' a termination of the campus greensward, and a visual connection to Escambia Bay beyond."
Steven M. Goldberg, FAIA

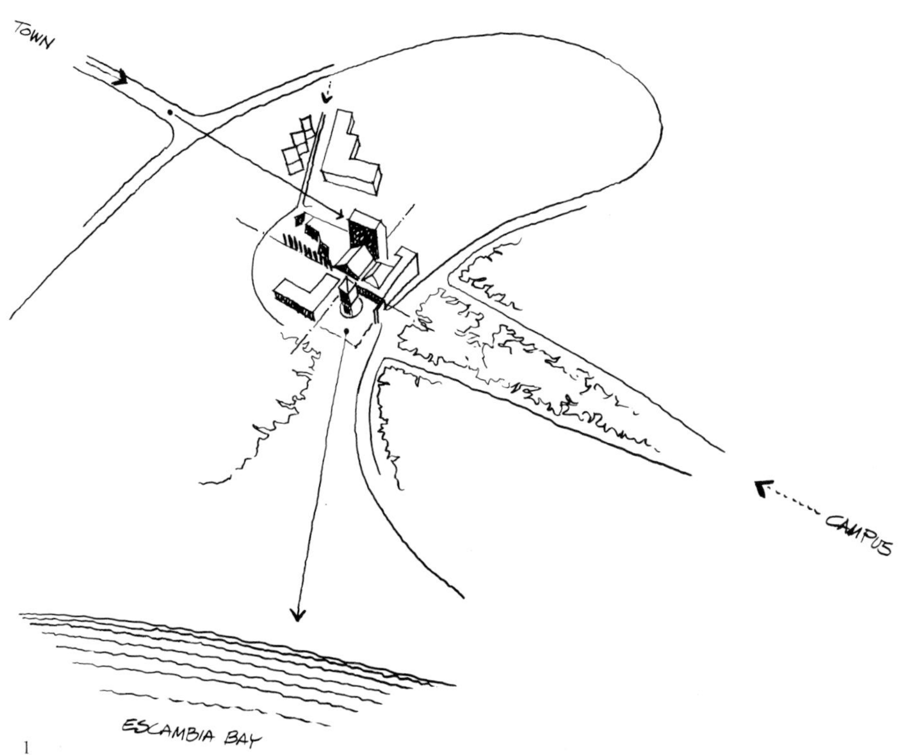

1

2

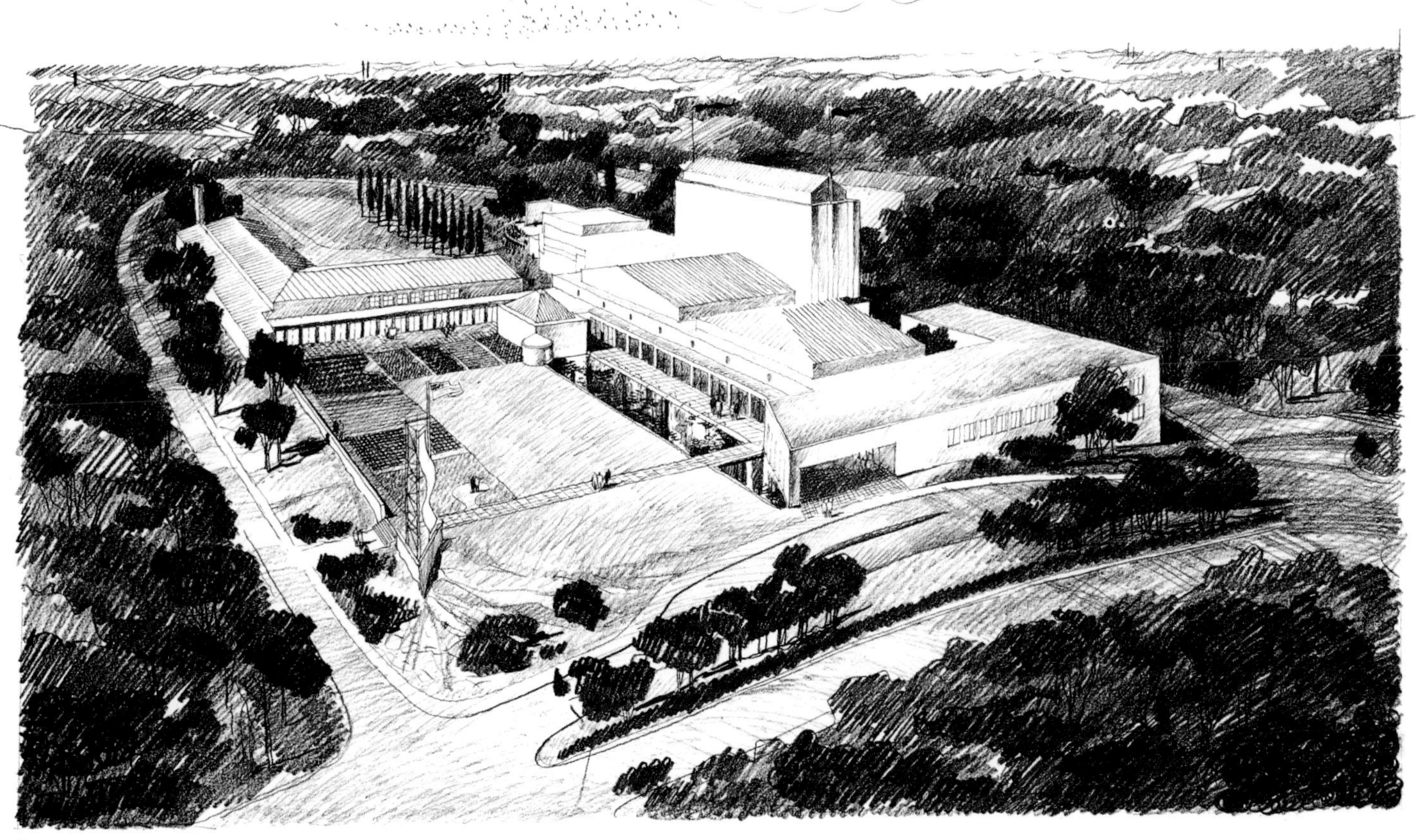

3

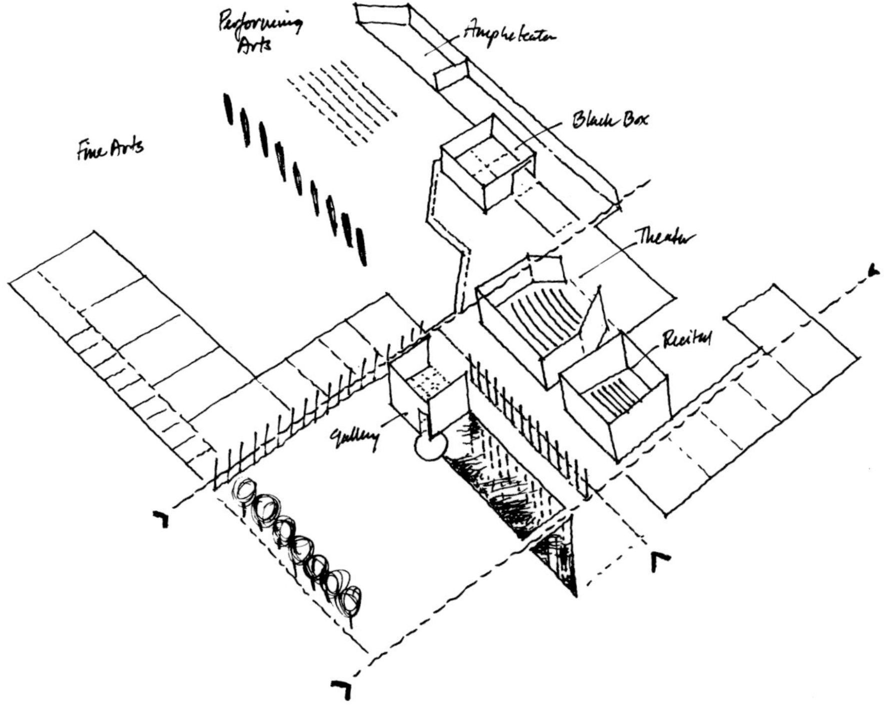

4

1 Site plan
2 View of entry court from the north-east
3 Aerial sketch of the complex
4 Conceptual diagram

5 North elevation
6 View of entry court from the north-east
7 View of gallery and performance halls
8 Entry lobby with gallery in the foreground

5

6

7

8

1 Main lobby
2 Gallery
3 Concert theater
4 Proscenium theater
5 Rehearsal hall
6 Library
7 Classroom
8 Practice rooms
9 Scene shop
10 Costume shop
11 Experimental theater
12 Office
13 Lobby
14 Green room
15 Dressing room
16 Gallery workroom
17 Studio
18 Darkroom

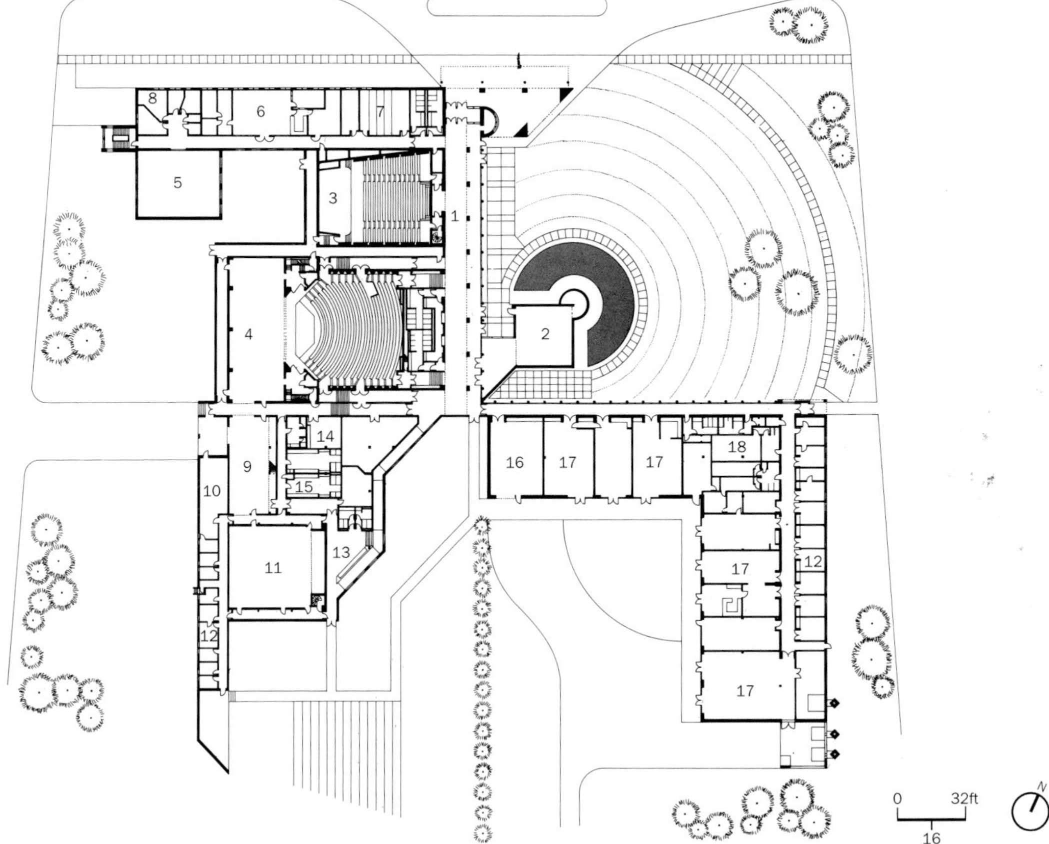

9

10

11

12

9 Floor plan
10 View from the west
11 Entry lobby
12 Recital hall

Onondaga County Convention Center

Design/Completion 1989/1992
Syracuse, New York
County of Onondaga/New York State Urban Development Corporation
210,000 square feet
Brick and aluminum curtain wall, limestone entry, aluminum roofing, terrazzo floors, concrete block, plaster and wood panel walls

The Onondaga County Convention Center is part of a Mitchell/Giurgola master plan for downtown Syracuse which includes the Civic Center theaters, War Memorial and arena, new and existing hotels, and parking. The master plan develops a precinct for public events in the center of Syracuse.

The pedestrian scale of downtown is reinforced by bridges and underground connections between the Convention Center, War Memorial, existing garages, a new parking garage, and a future hotel site. To address this pedestrian emphasis, the ballroom and meeting rooms are below grade and the exhibition halls are recessed from public lobbies to minimize overall building bulk.

Sidewalk elevations are familiar in color and scale and reveal public activities to passers-by. The high volume of the 65,000-square-foot exhibition space is white and provides a backdrop for the aluminum vault of the main lobby.

"The building should provide significant public rooms that enhance convention activities but, more importantly, are places to be enjoyed by the community." Steven M. Goldberg, FAIA

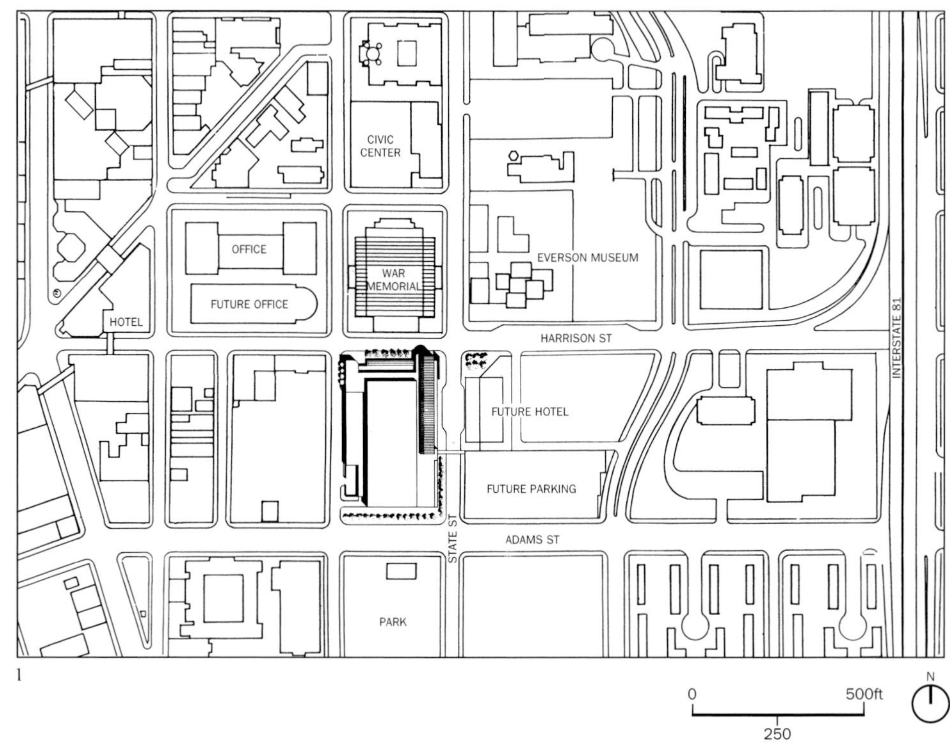

1

2

1 Site plan
2 Entry detail
3 Master plan/urban connections diagram
4 Main entry at north-east corner

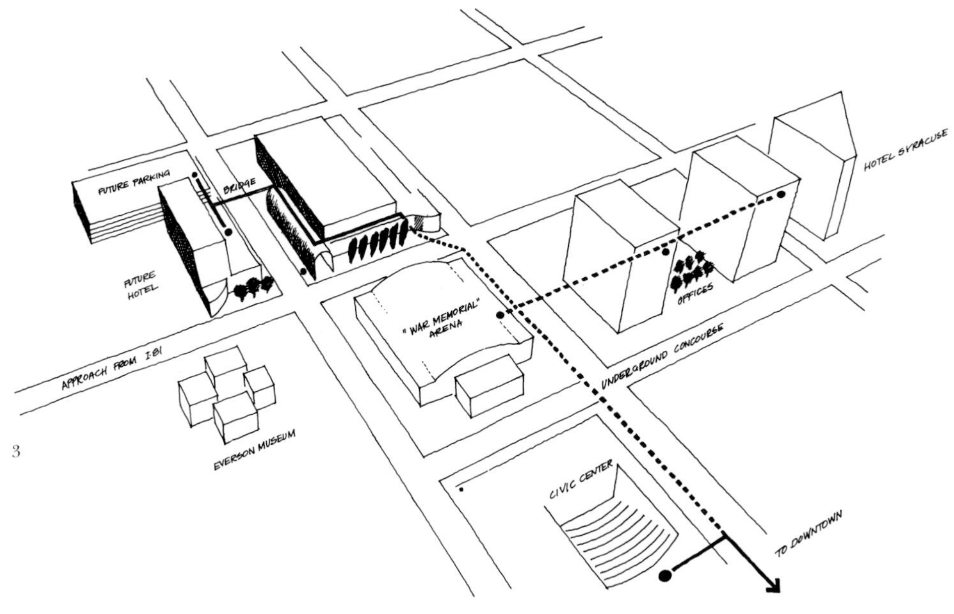

3

4

5 Main lobby wing at night
6 Aerial view of the complex
7 Main entry and drop-off

5

6

7

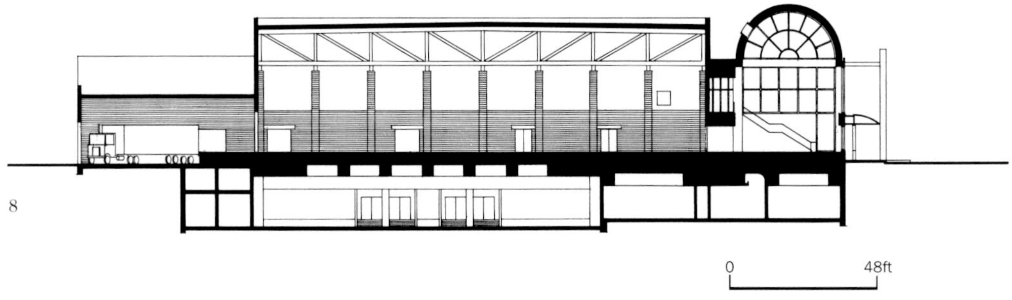

8

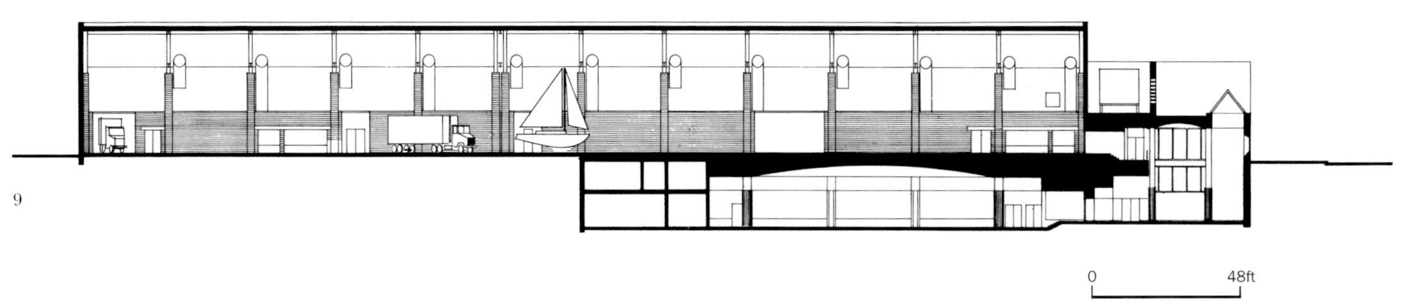

9

10

11

12

8 East–west section looking north
9 North–south section looking west
10 Main exhibit pre-function space
11 Pedestrian bridge from parking garage to main lobby
12 Public stair to administration offices

13 Main lobby and pre-function space
14 Ballroom pre-function space

13

14

15

16

15 Below grade pedestrian concourse to arena across the street
16 Exhibition hall with auditorium seating arrangement
17 Ballroom set up for a wedding

17

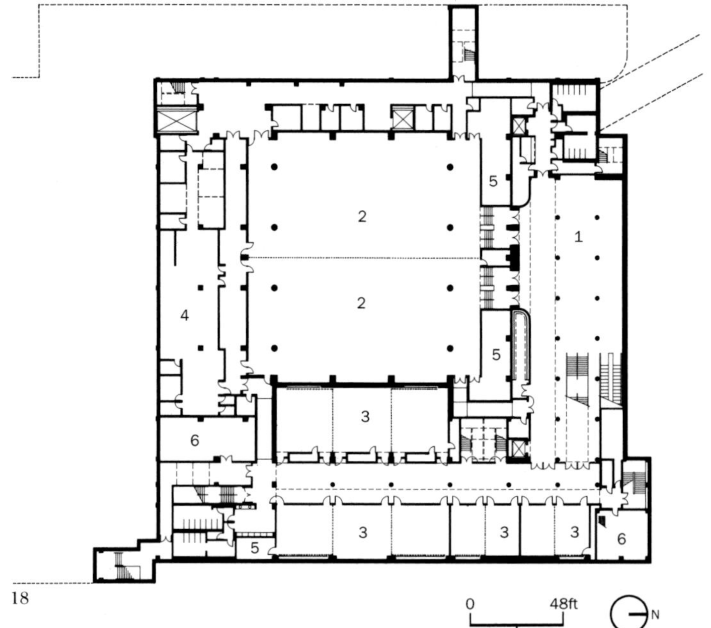

18

1 Banquet pre-function
2 Banquet hall
3 Meeting room
4 Kitchen
5 Storage
6 Mechanical

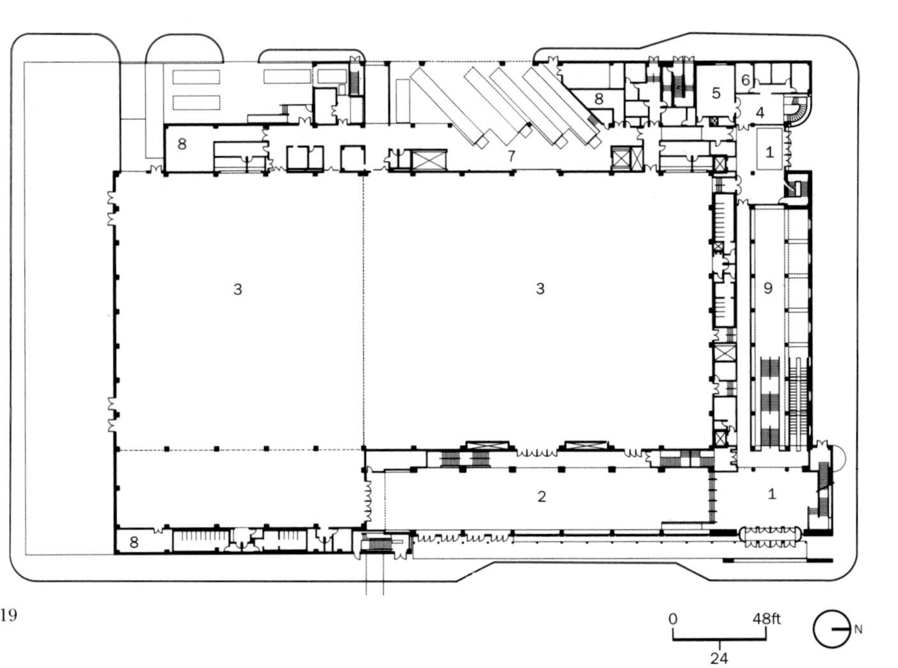

19

1 Lobby
2 Exhibition pre-function
3 Exhibition hall
4 Reception
5 Meeting room
6 Office
7 Loading dock
8 Storage
9 Open to below

18 Lower level plan
19 Ground level plan
20 Reception stair

20

Harlem International Trade Center

Design/Completion 1993/1998
Harlem, New York
Harlem International Trade Center Corporation/
New York State Development Corporation
Associate architects: Roberta Washington Architect, PC
and URS Consultants, Inc.
400,000 square feet
Stone and metal panels, curtain wall, glass block, stone paving

The Harlem International Trade Center was conceived as a place where trade missions from developing countries seeking to cultivate trade with the United States could focus their efforts. The center also serves Americans who are interested in trading in Africa, the Caribbean and Latin America.

Located in one of six federal Empowerment Zones on 125th Street in Harlem, the site offers spectacular views across Central Park to midtown Manhattan. The as-of-right building complex consists of a 22-story office tower, meeting and conference rooms, hotel, banquet rooms, exhibition spaces, restaurants, a business club, new and renovated retail space, and parking.

The design solution enhances the vitality of 125th Street by strongly celebrating public activity at the street level.

"Our goal was to challenge the ubiquitous 'wedding cake' solution to zoning restrictions and create a distinct silhouette along the city's skyline which animates the public and festive aspects of the program." Mark Markiewicz, AIA

1

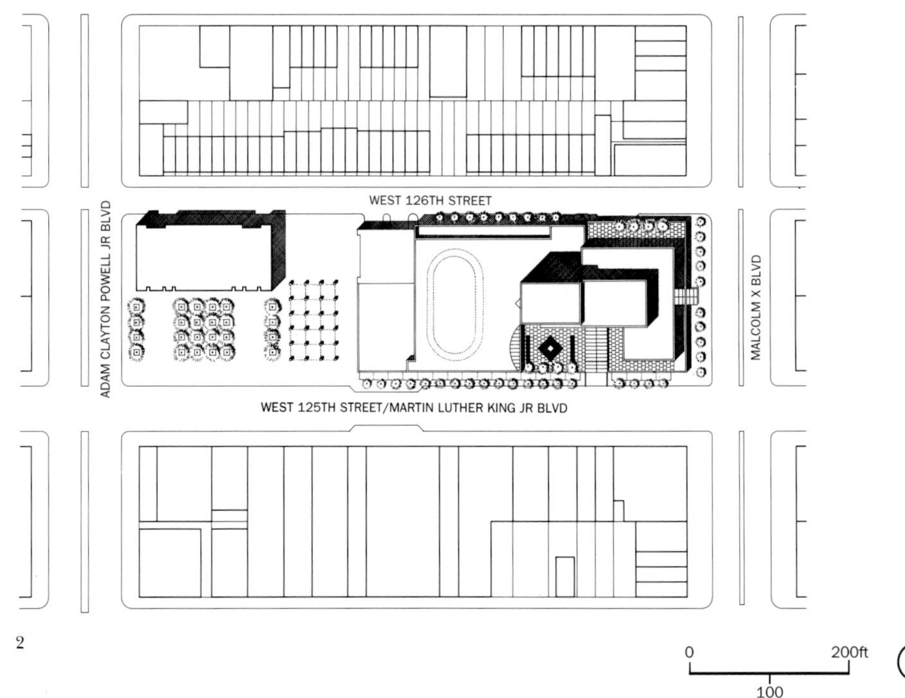

2

1 Sketch of completed building
2 Site plan
3 View looking east along 125th Street

3

4 East–west section with program distribution
5 Panorama of Harlem seen across Central Park
6 South elevation along 125th Street
7&8 Preliminary sketches
9 View looking north-west along Lenox Avenue

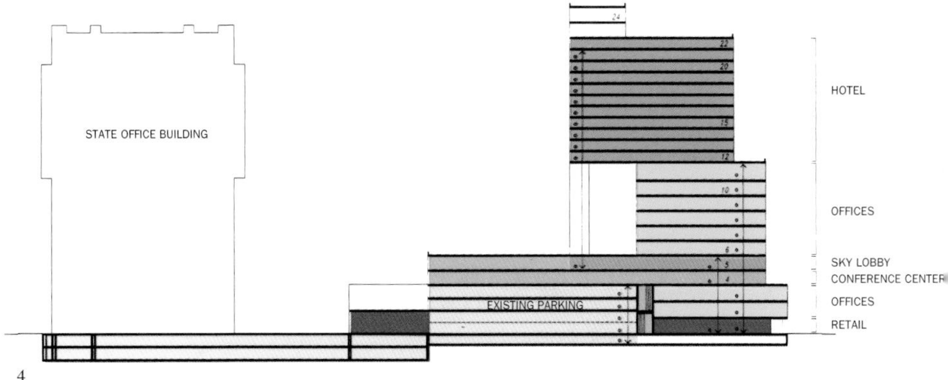

4

5

6

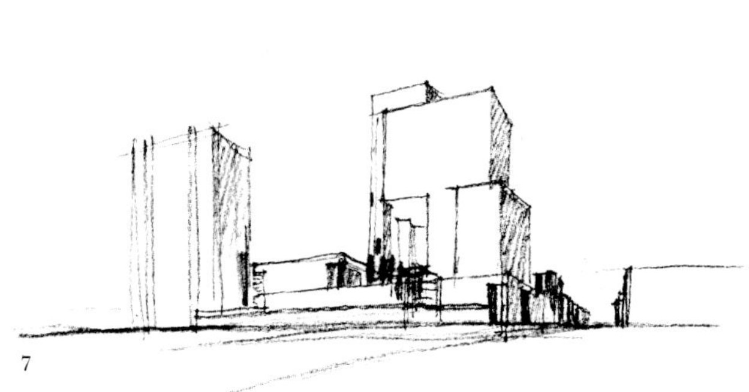
7

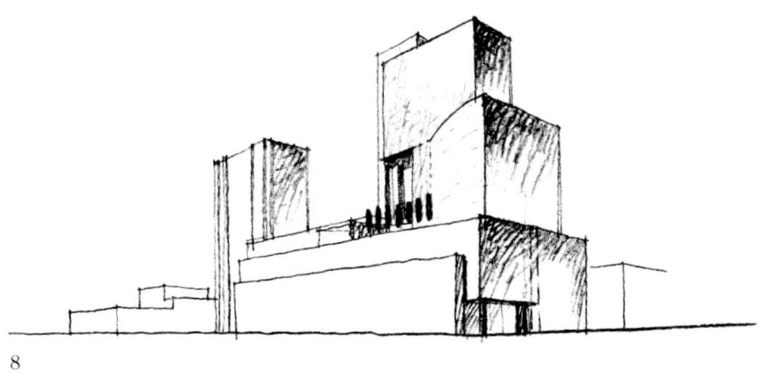
8

9

RESEARCH/STUDY PLACES

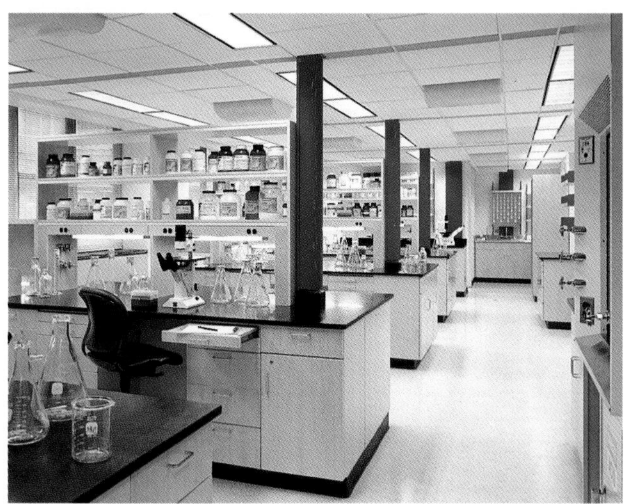

George M. Low Center for Industrial Innovation, Rensselaer Polytechnic Institute

Design/Completion 1982/1987
Troy, New York
200,000 square feet
Cast-in-place concrete with red brick and white brick exterior

The Center for Industrial Innovation is a facility for the interaction of academic research and industrial application in new high-technology disciplines. The program consists of laboratories and offices for three "sectors" derived from existing academic groups: microelectronics, computer-aided design, and manufacturing technology. Laboratories, offices, and seminar/conference facilities for the use of visiting professionals from industry are part of the fourth sector—industrial innovation.

The center consists of three major building masses. A four-story portion, similar in scale to the older buildings nearby and housing high-bay spaces with conference and seminar rooms, is on the north side of the campus lawn. A seven-story central element consists of two flexible laboratory blocks flanking a vertical "utility corridor" ringed with offices.

"Our goal was to facilitate interaction between multi-disciplinary research groups and private industry, while accommodating the fast-moving changes in technology." Jan Keane, FAIA

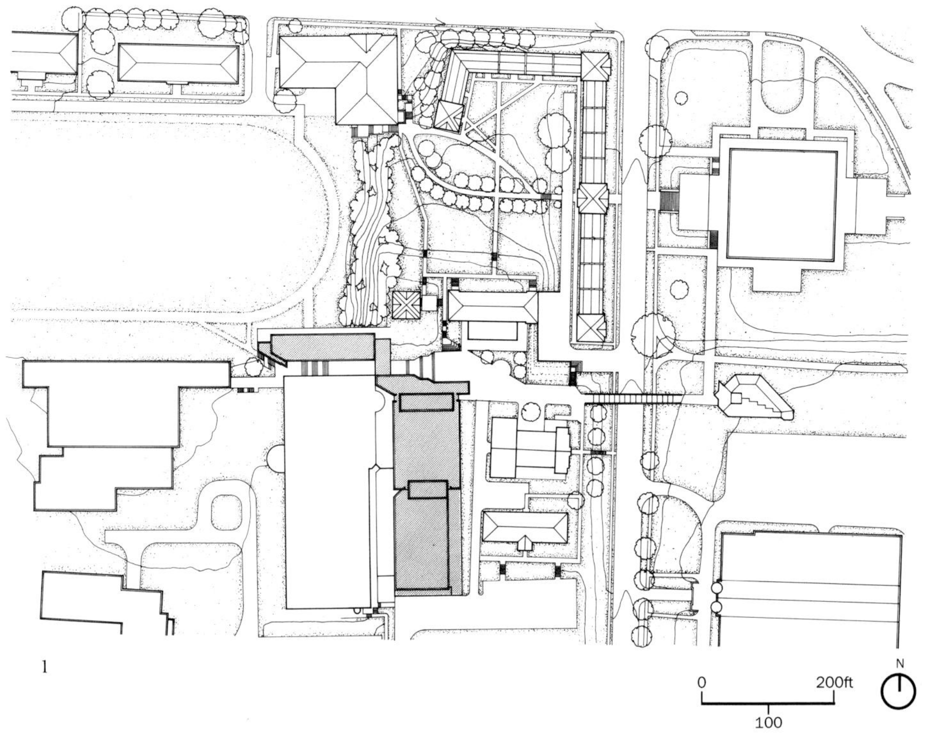

1

2

1 Site plan
2 East elevation
3 East elevation facing campus walk

GEORGE M. LOW
CENTER FOR INDUSTRIAL INNOVATION
Campus Notices

3

4 Siting/campus circulation diagram
5 East elevation
6 Building diagram
7 North elevation of high-bay wing

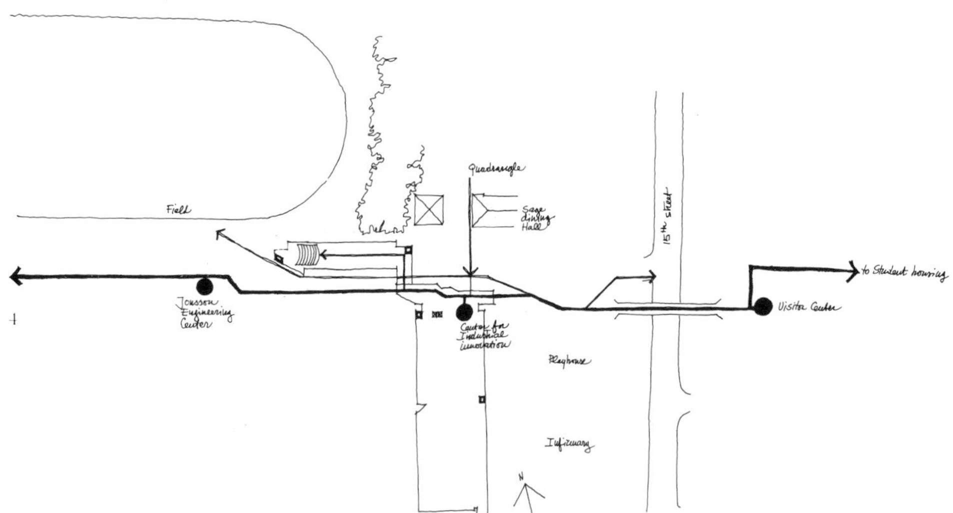

4

5

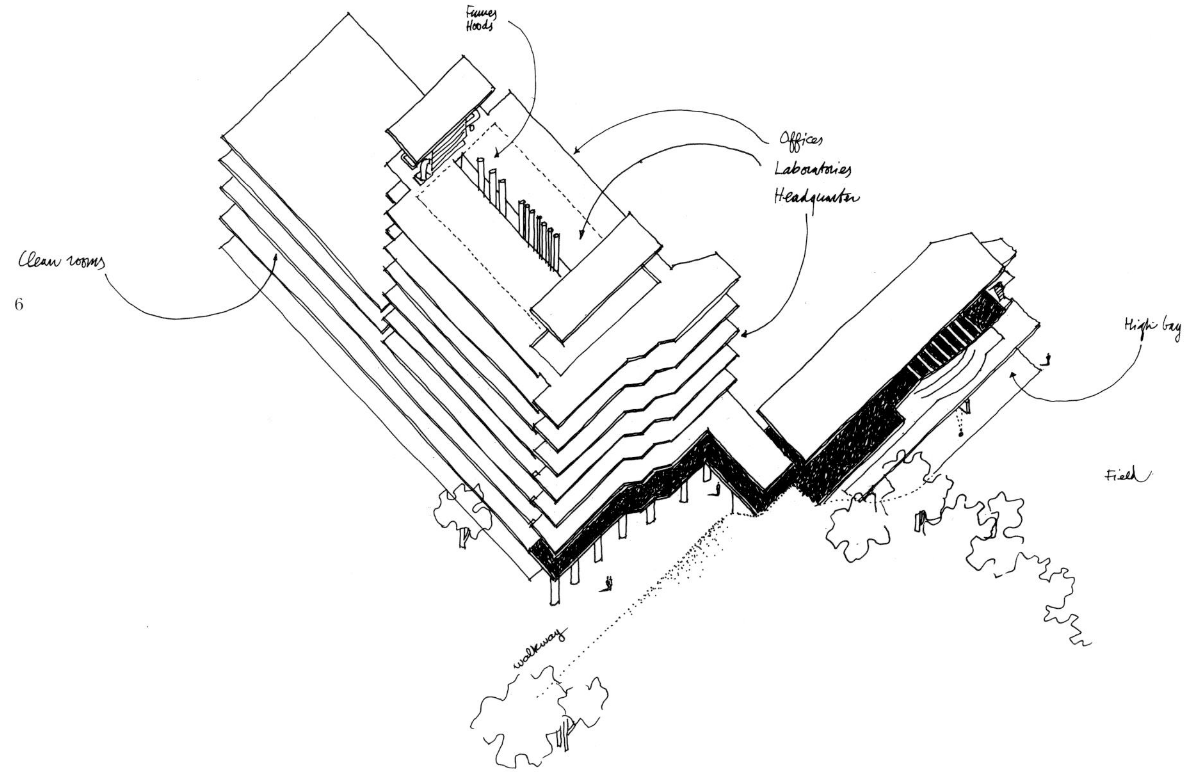
Fumes Hoods
Offices
Laboratories
Headquarter
Clean rooms
High bay
Field
walkway

6

7

1 Secretary
2 Office
3 Conference room
4 Classroom
5 Lecture hall
6 Computer room
7 Lobby
8 Mechanical
9 Campus walkway

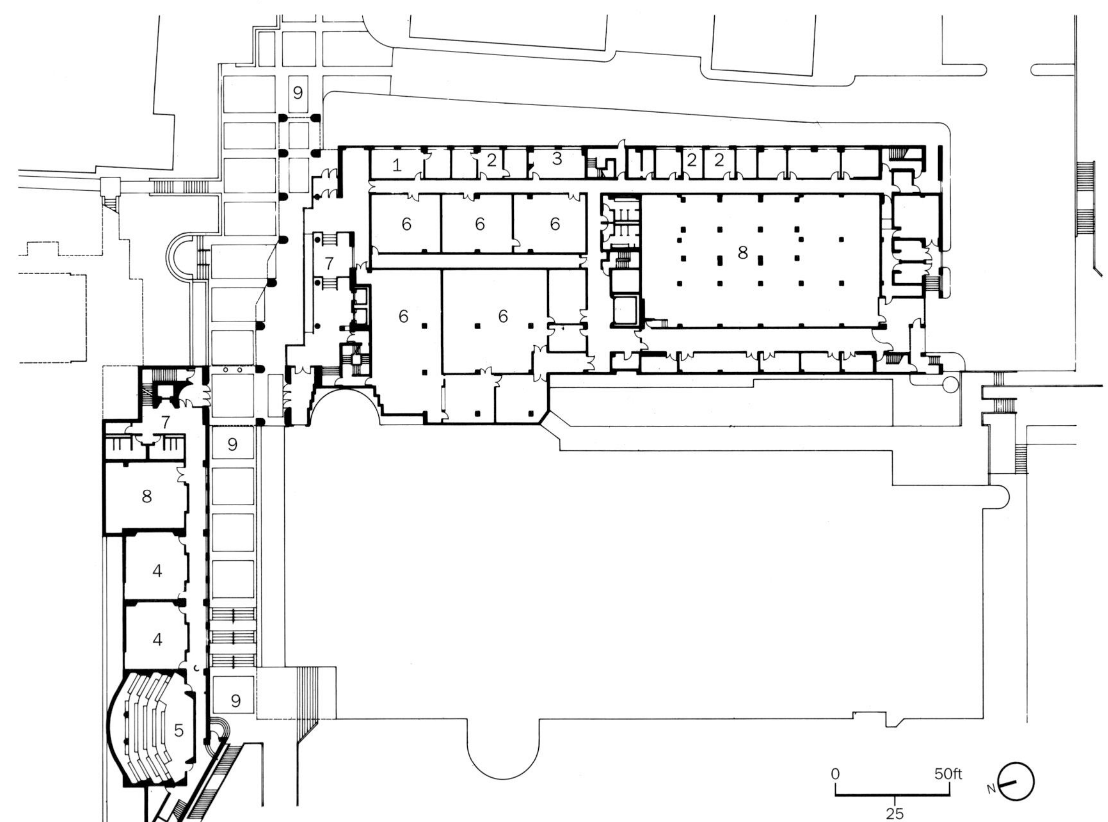

8

1 Laboratory
2 Secretary
3 Office
4 Conference room
5 Clean room
6 Classroom
7 Lecture hall

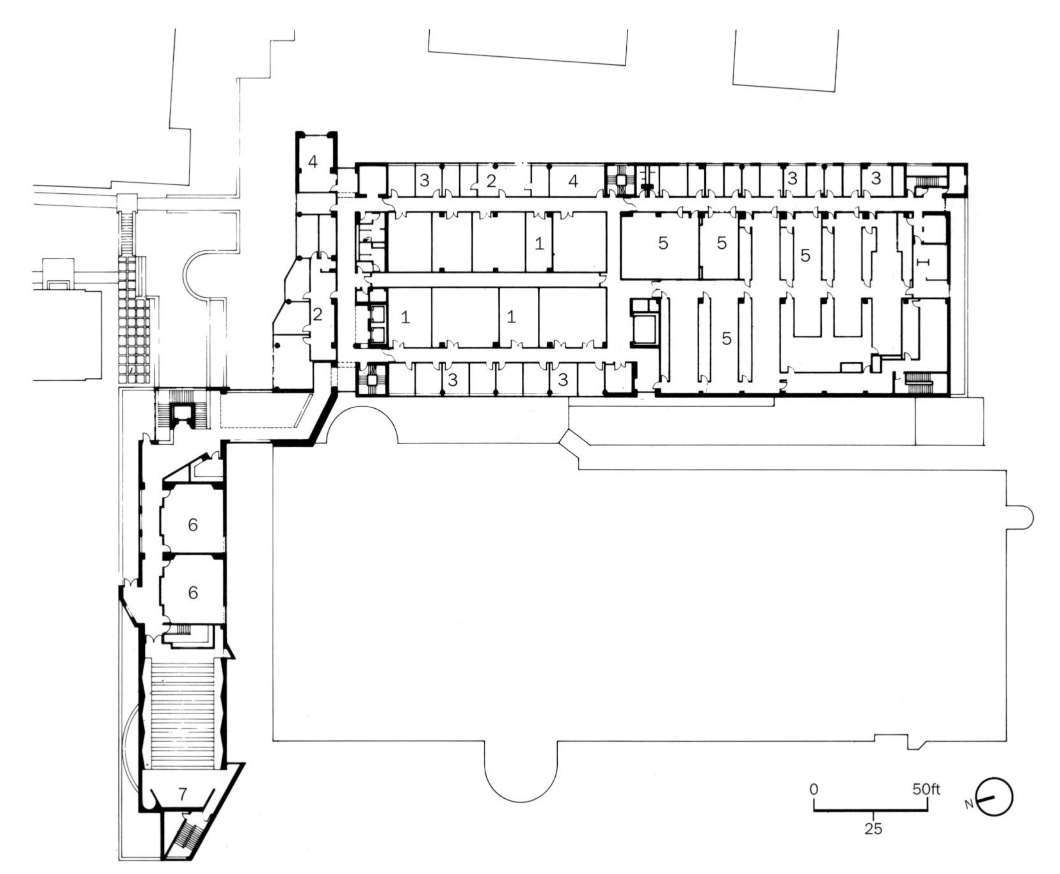

9

8 Third level plan
9 Fourth level plan
10 Ground-floor lobby with tile mural by Lin Utzon
11 View from the north-west

10

11

12

13

12 Typical engineering laboratory
13 Semi-conductor manufacturing "cleanroom"
14 High-bay area

14

Outpatient Care Center

Design/Completion 1986/1990
Los Angeles, California
The University of California at Los Angeles
Associate architect: Daniel, Mann, Johnson & Mendenhall
380,000 square feet
Precast concrete with panels of green slate, glass block, painted metal roof, aluminum windows

The Outpatient Care Center is predicated on the dual notions that medical staff can be more productive if private clinics are nearby, and the ambulatory patient will be more pleasantly served in a "low barrier," less institutional environment.

The project is the centerpiece of a three-building complex, including an outpatient facility, medical office building, and health clinics, all oriented around a pedestrian and vehicular entry court. The massing of the building provides a strong "frame" for the court, while simultaneously accommodating existing circulation routes with its dramatic stepped east end.

An outdoor pediatric play area and gardens located between the complex and adjacent parking garage form a spine of active green space.

The interior is organized around a single-loaded corridor with generous bay windows overlooking the entry court. Clinic waiting areas open to the inside of this daylit corridor.

"The scale, colors and the brightness of glass are intended to convey a sense of optimism to the visiting patient." Mark Markiewicz, AIA

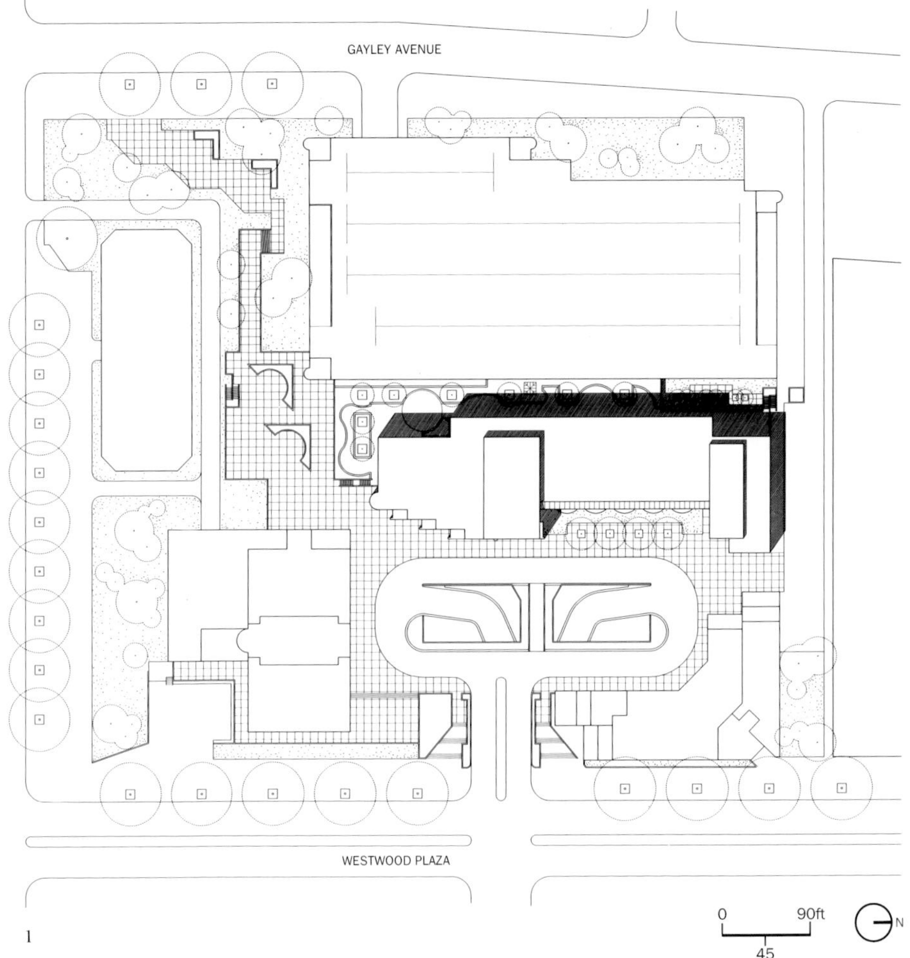

1 Site plan
2 View from the east
3 Conference room

2

3

4 East elevation
5 South-east corner
6 Ground-floor plan
7 Entry tower with public circulation bay windows

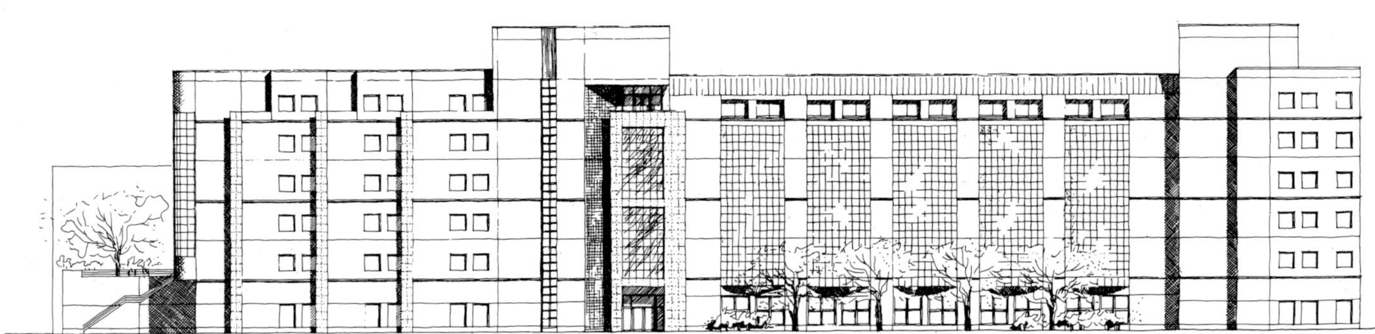

4

5

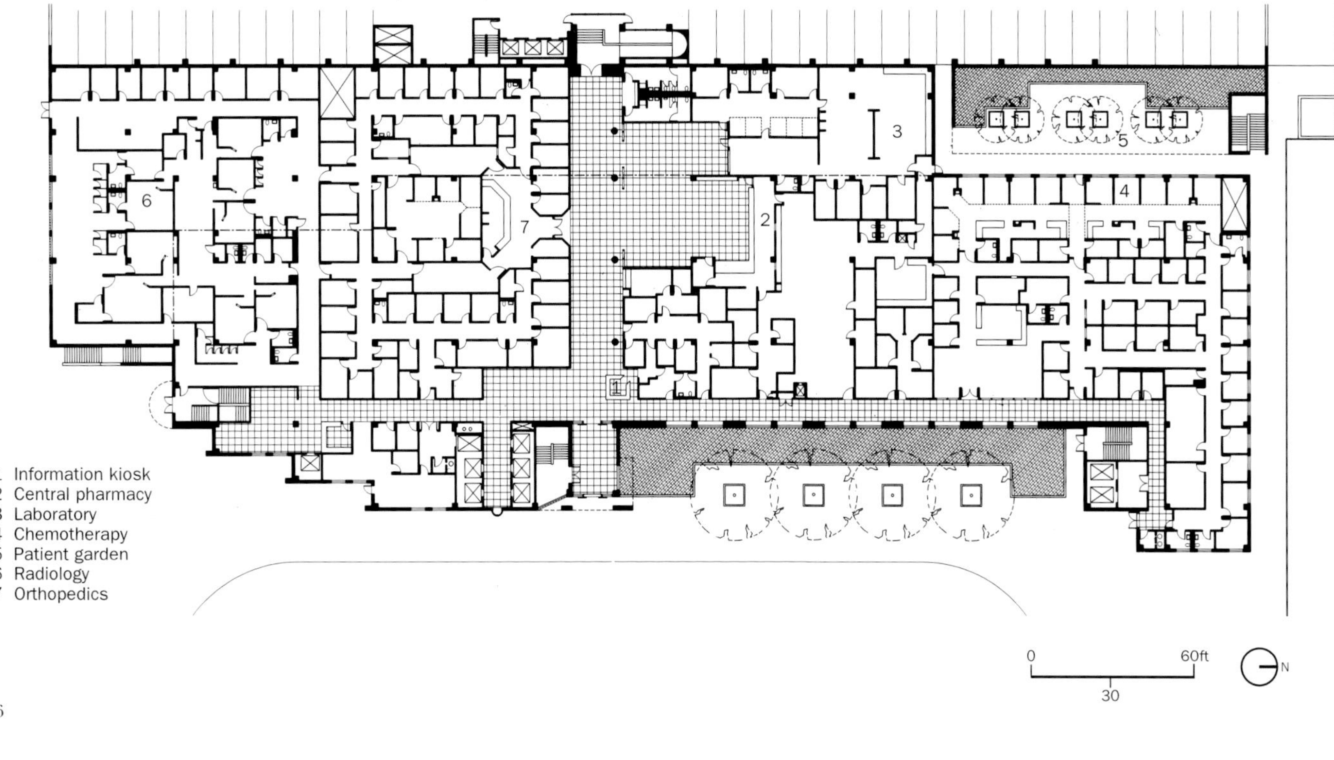
1 Information kiosk
2 Central pharmacy
3 Laboratory
4 Chemotherapy
5 Patient garden
6 Radiology
7 Orthopedics
0
60ft
30
N

6

7

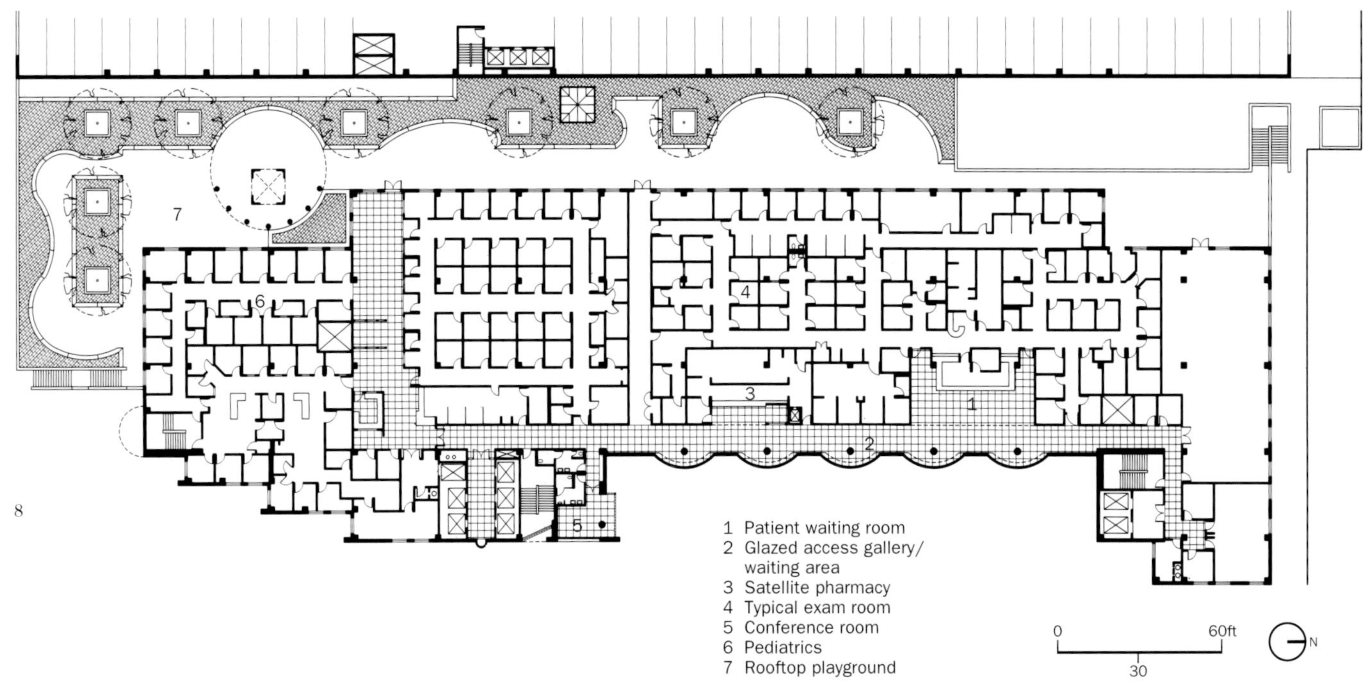
1 Patient waiting room
2 Glazed access gallery/ waiting area
3 Satellite pharmacy
4 Typical exam room
5 Conference room
6 Pediatrics
7 Rooftop playground
0
60ft
30
N

8

9

8 Second-floor plan
9 Main entry lobby, accessible from rear parking
10 Public circulation to clinics

10

Revelle College Sciences Building

Design/Completion 1988/1993
LaJolla, California
University of California at San Diego
Associate architect: Austin Hansen Fehlman
183,000 square feet
Precast concrete panels, teak windows, glass block, perforated metal awnings

The new sciences building houses laboratories and support facilities for the departments of biology and chemistry. The main body of the building was placed to take advantage of its prominence as a pedestrian entry to an expanding campus. The scheme carries on the tradition of courtyards and completes a delightful outdoor room.

In its current configuration, each department occupies half of the building with flexibility for future expansion. It provides laboratory space for 40 investigative groups with associated conference and seminar space. Animal quarters and neuro-muscular research facilities are located at the basement level to provide secure and vibration-free space. Two types of sunshades frame the view and offer protection.

"The design reflects the open spirit of the campus as characterized by intense greenery, abundant sunlight and the powerful presence of the Pacific Ocean. The large-scale, colorful exterior materials were selected to shine in the sunny Southern California climate."
Mark Markiewicz, AIA

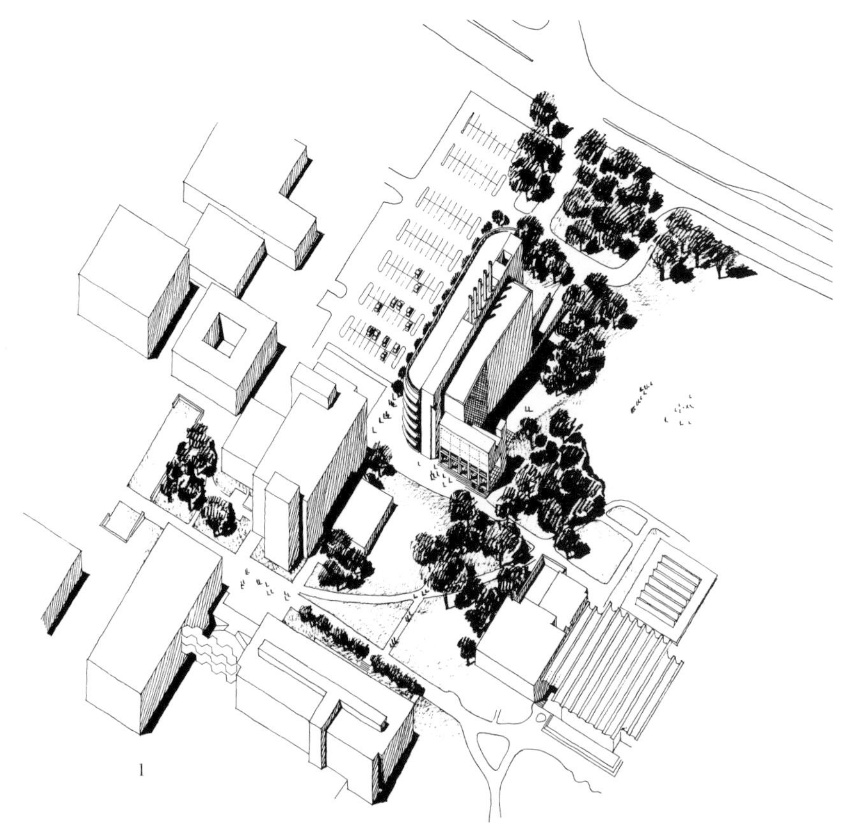

1

2

3

4

1 Building in context
2 Sciences building completes the north facade of the courtyard
3 East facade seen from the campus
4 View from the terrace to the Pacific Ocean

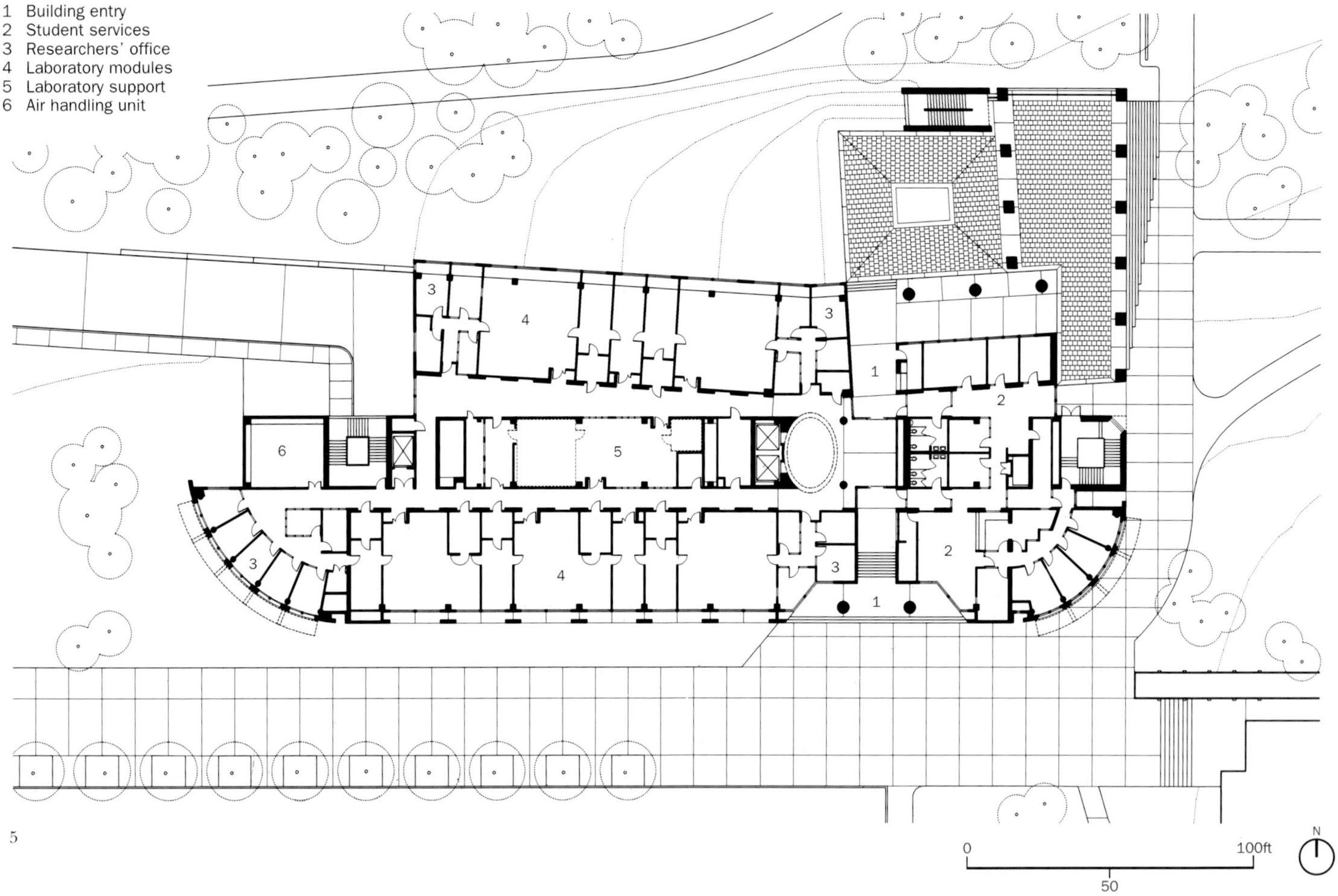

1 Building entry
2 Student services
3 Researchers' office
4 Laboratory modules
5 Laboratory support
6 Air handling unit

0 100ft
50
N

5

6

5 Ground-floor plan
6 East facade and courtyard
7 View from sports fields to the north-west
8 Entry portico

7

8

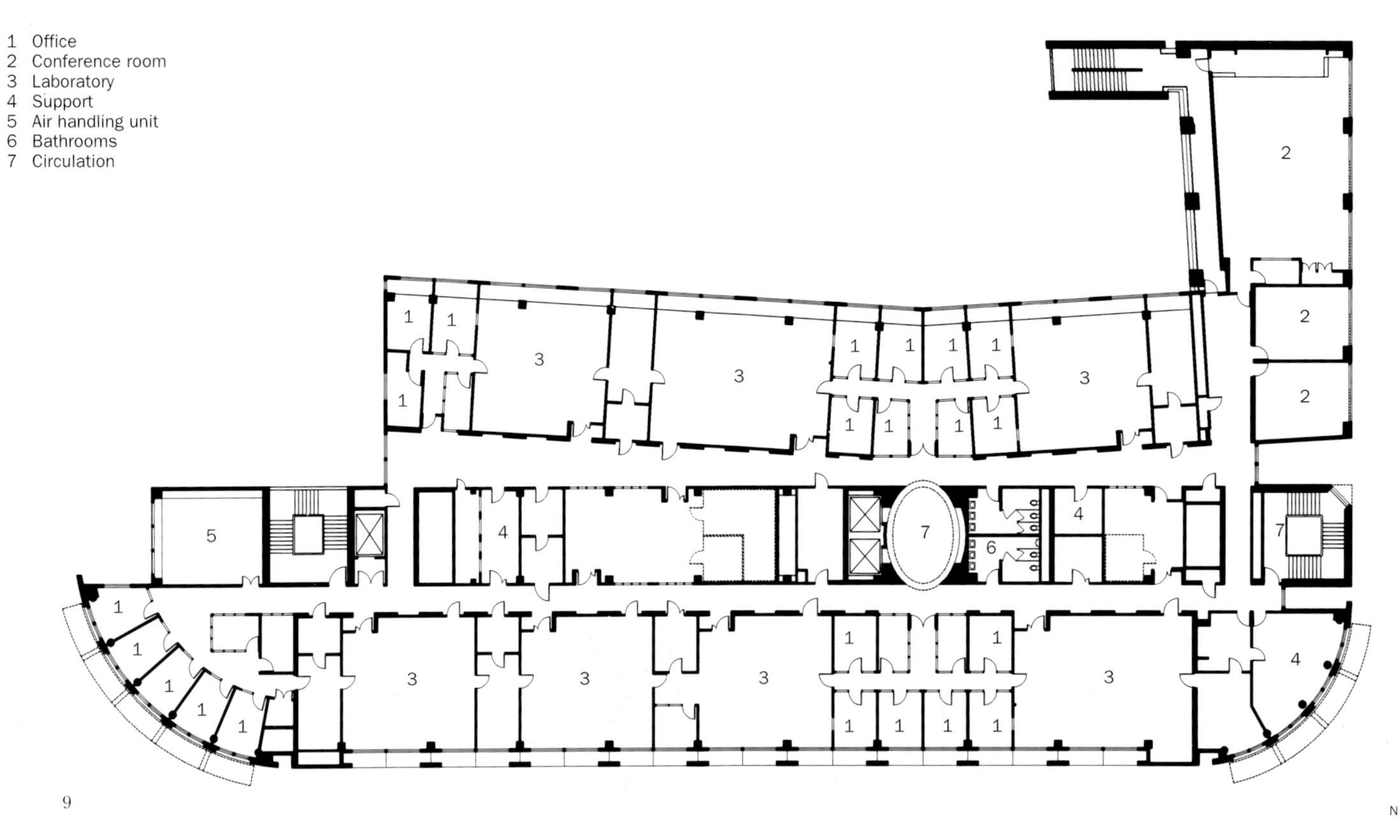
1 Office
2 Conference room
3 Laboratory
4 Support
5 Air handling unit
6 Bathrooms
7 Circulation
0
50
100ft
N

9

10

9 Third-floor plan
10 Detail of sun shades
11 Conference room
12 Typical laboratory
13 Elevator lobby

11

12

13

Life Sciences Building

Design/Completion 1988/1993–95
Summit, New Jersey
Ciba Pharmaceuticals Division
440,000 square feet
Precast concrete, aluminum curtain wall, stone accents of marble, granite and green slate

The new Life Sciences Building consolidates research on a single R&D campus for the first time. The stepped plan organizes a series of shared outdoor spaces to create a unified research area which is open and pedestrian in scale. The building is designed on a modular grid to accommodate a variety of disciplines and to facilitate adaptation.

To make the laboratories both flexible and open, and to promote interaction, there are very few dividing walls. The perimeter corridors have glazing into the labs above desk-height and large windows to the outside, or are open into two interior covered atria. At both ends of these covered courts are circulation nodes with meeting rooms, stairs, elevators, and coffee break areas. The Ciba research group believes that new ideas in research often result from informal interaction.

The use of 88-foot trusses allows column-free laboratories with 8-foot interstices above. Services drop to the labs through openings in the concrete ceiling.

"Creating a flexible and interactive environment for the innovative research at Ciba informed our design from the outset." Jan Keane, FAIA

1

2

1 Site plan
2 Coffee break area
3 East elevation/coffee break area

3

4 View of east entry
5 View of south facade
6 Entry detail
7 Window detail

4

5

6

7

8 First-floor plan
9 Second- and third-floor plan
10 Fountain view axial

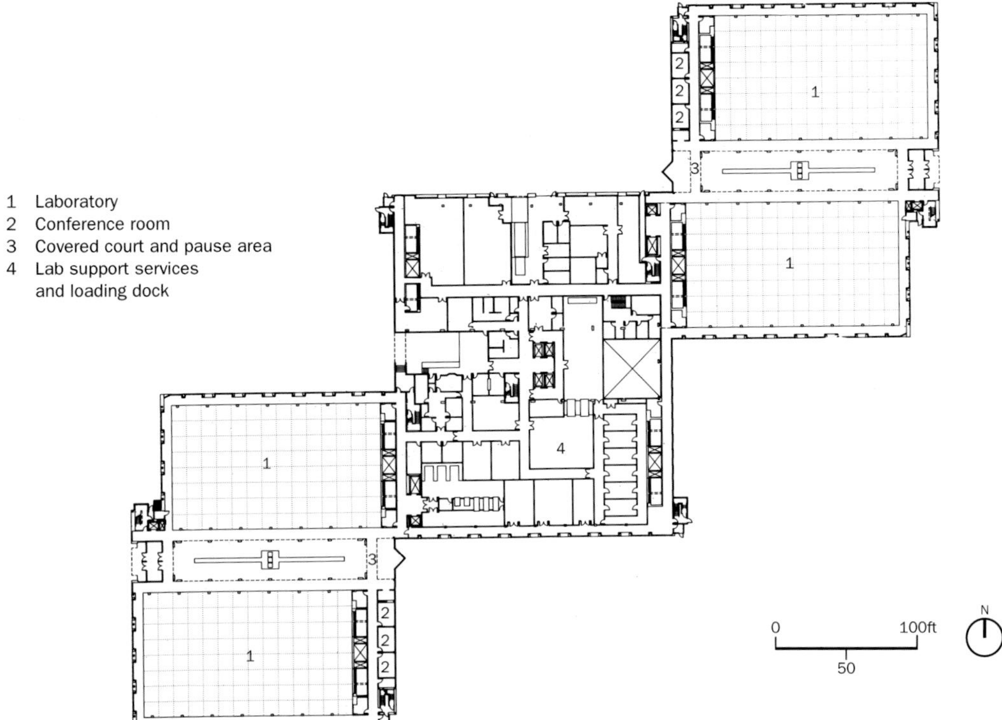

8

1 Laboratory
2 Conference room
3 Pause area
4 In vivo study area
5 Open to below

0 50 100ft

N

9

10

11

11 View across atrium
12 Lounge/coffee break area
13 Corridor to the laboratories
14 Conference room

12

13

14

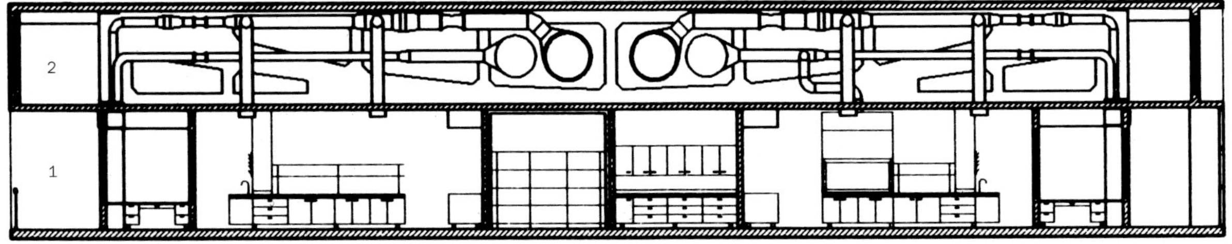

1 Laboratory floor
2 Interstitial space

0 25ft
10
N

15

15 Laboratory floor and interstitial space section
16 Interstitial bay
17 Typical split bench laboratory
18 Building section
19&20 Typical bench laboratory

16

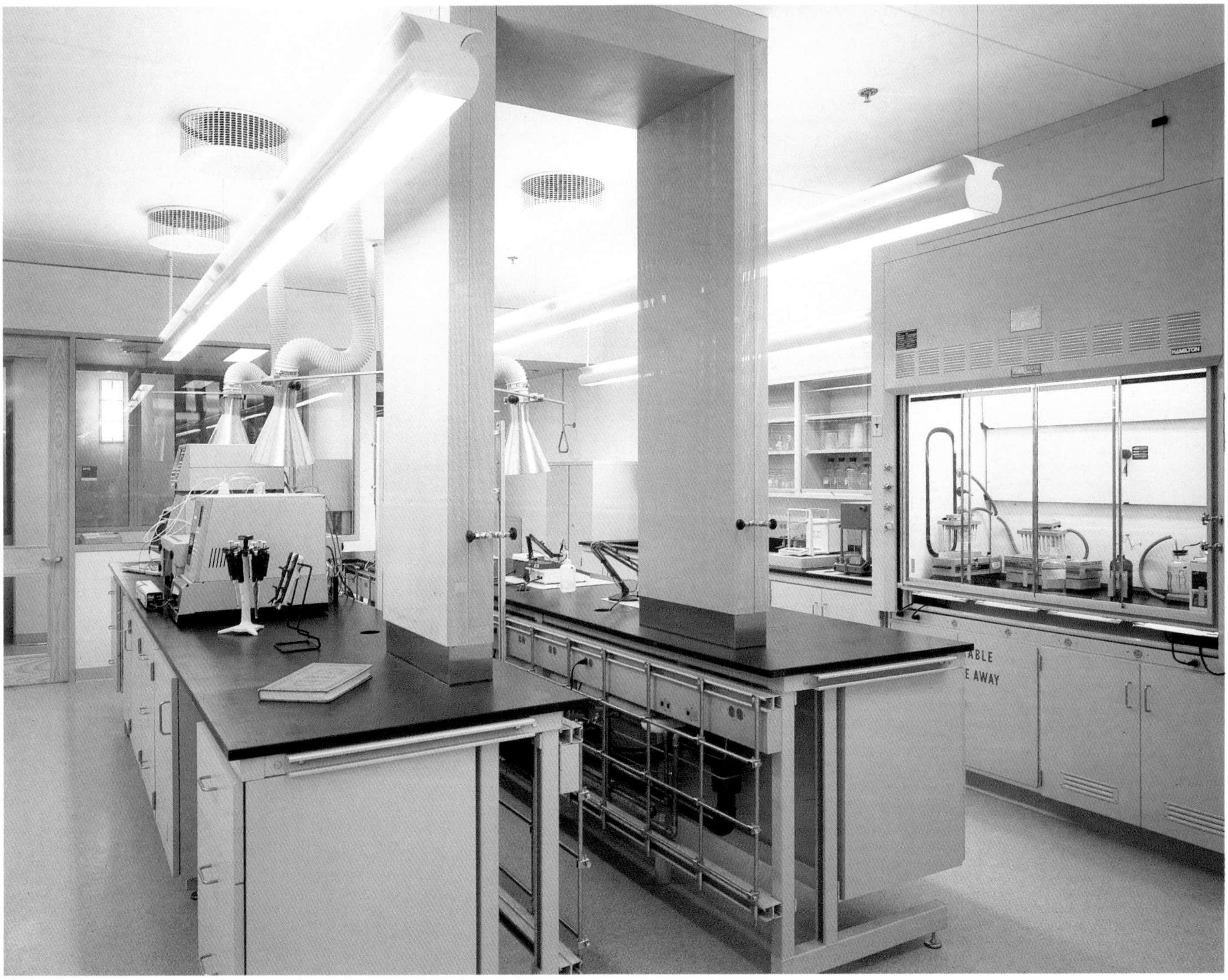

17

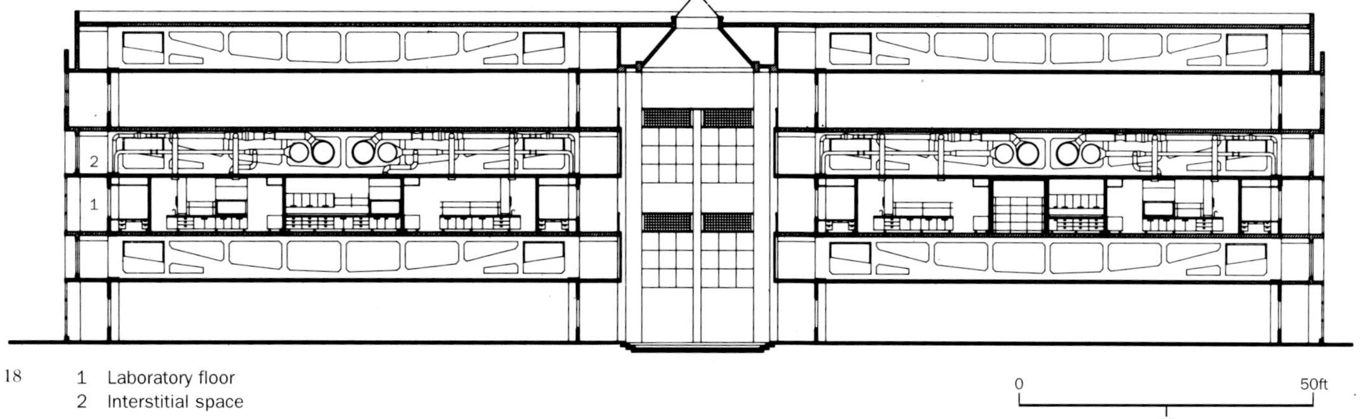

18 1 Laboratory floor
2 Interstitial space

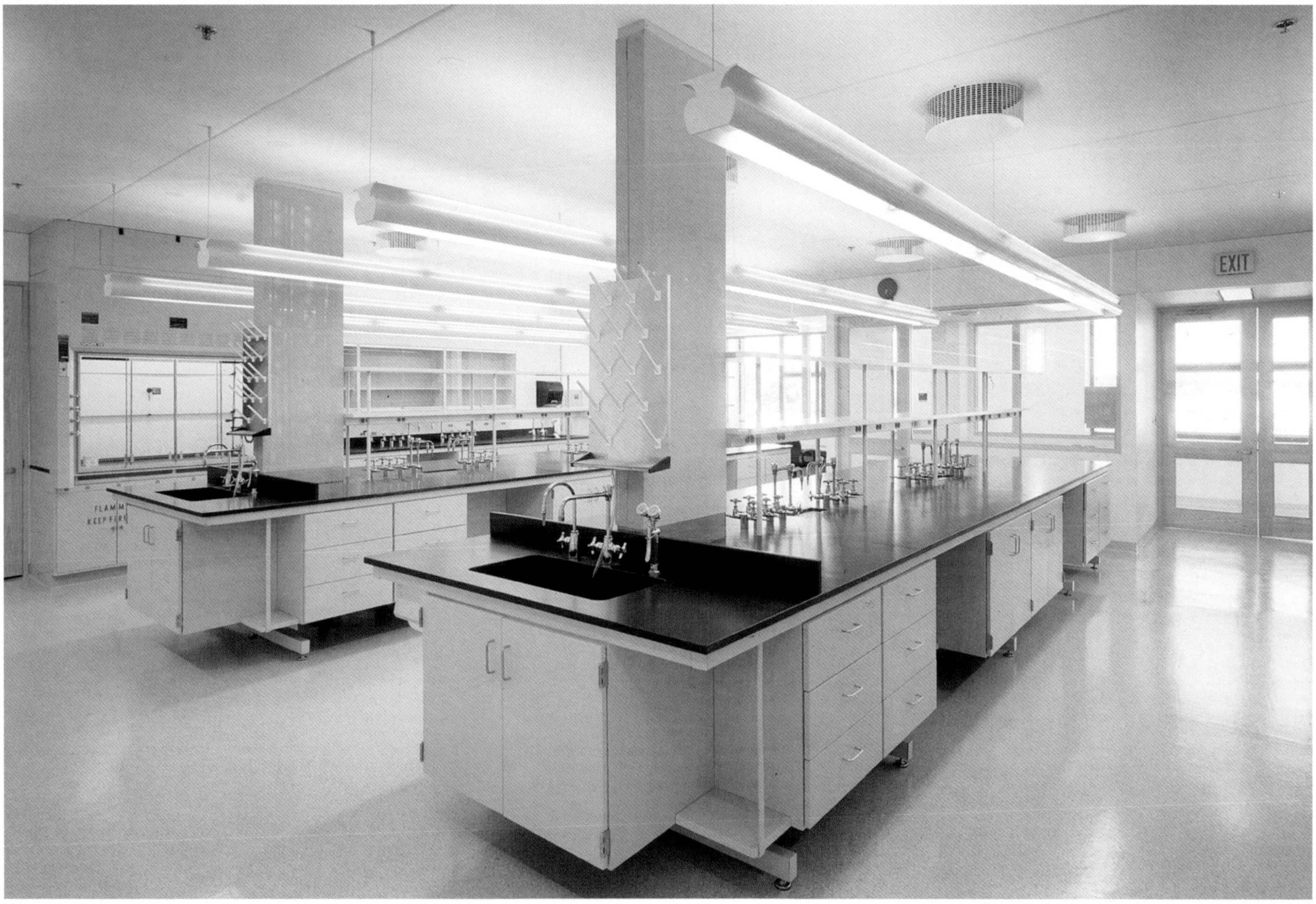

19

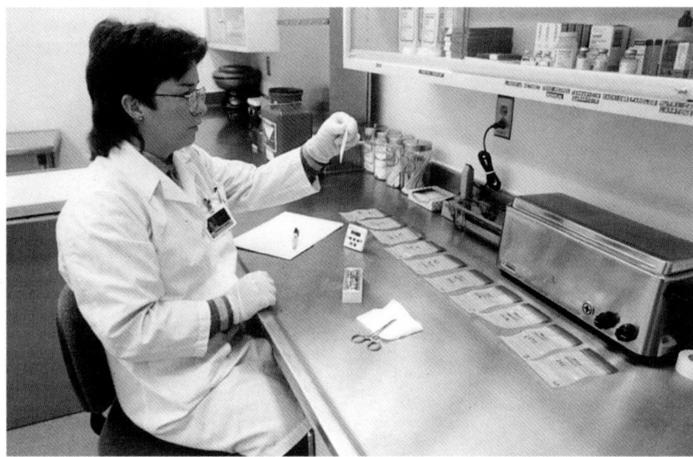

20

Ceramics Corridor Innovation Center, Corning

Design/Completion 1990/1992
Corning, New York
Alfred Technology Resources Inc./New York State Urban Development Corporation
40,000 square feet
Ground face concrete block, metal panels, windows and skylights

Two new incubator facilities encourage economic development along the "corridor" between Alfred and Corning in New York's southern tier and support the development of high-technology ceramics. Both buildings can accommodate approximately 12 start-up companies. In addition to laboratory space for research and production, each facility provides administrative offices for a director and secretaries, as well as a library, conference space, a computer room, and a lounge. A high-bay space in each facility is intended for large-scale shared equipment such as kilns.

The Corning facility is situated amidst cultivated land in a valley. The building consists of a long, single-story wing which contains the high-bay area and production/research facilities, and a smaller entry wing parallel to the road, which contains the common areas and administrative offices.

"Both the research wing and the administrative center respond to particular conditions of the site. The courtyard created by their juxtaposition focuses views to the valley beyond." John Kurtz, AIA

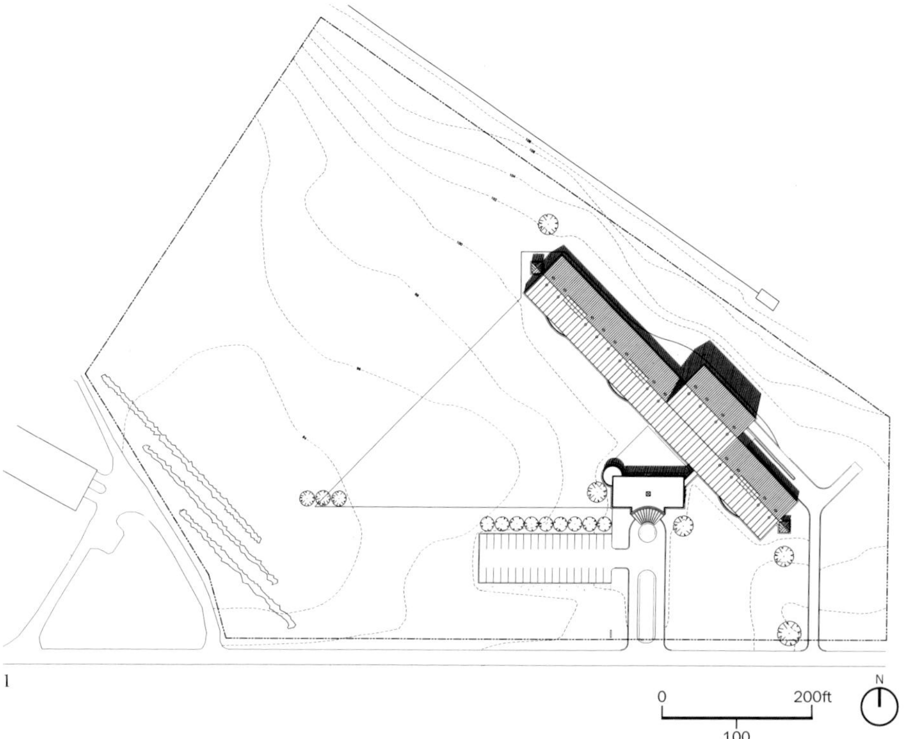

1

2

1 Site plan
2 Laboratory corridor with administration wing beyond
3 Conference room with laboratory wing beyond
4 Main entry

3

4

1 High bay
2 Production research
3 Office
4 Conference room
5 Library
6 Cafeteria
7 Lounge
8 Loading dock

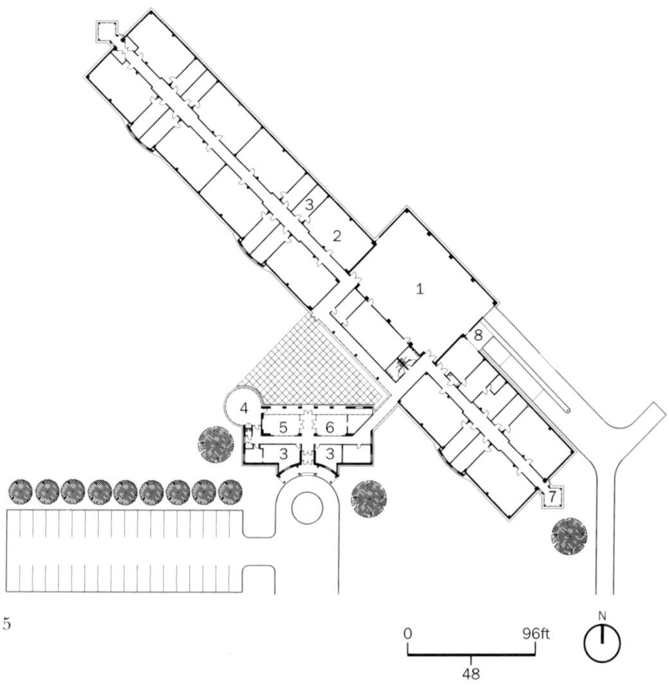

5

6

7

5 Floor plan
6 Central corridor
7 West elevation
8 Laboratory wing with lounge pavilion
9 Entry court

8

9

Ceramics Corridor Innovation Center, Alfred

Design/Completion 1990/1992
Alfred, New York
Alfred Technology Resources Inc./New York State Urban Development Corporation
30,000 square feet
Ground face concrete block
Metal panels, windows and skylights

One of two new "incubator" facilities for high-technology ceramics development, the Alfred site is located at the edge of a small embankment. Because the site is at a lower elevation than the roadway, the entry and main public spaces of this two-story building are oriented toward the wooded hills in the distance.

Tenant research/production space is organized on a 12' x 30' rental module flanking a double-loaded corridor. Additional programmed spaces include administrative offices, a six-module high-bay area, public-use rooms, a library, and a lounge.

The exterior of the building is clad in white ground face concrete block with gray accents; the windows and roof are painted metal. Shafts through the second floor for fume hood and heat exhaust ductwork are located at each module in tenant work areas. The corridor attic, which extends the length of the building, contains exhaust fans and other mechanical equipment.

"As small companies grow and move on, one hopes they will take with them not only their new technology, but also a commitment to the merits of good design."
Jan Keane, FAIA

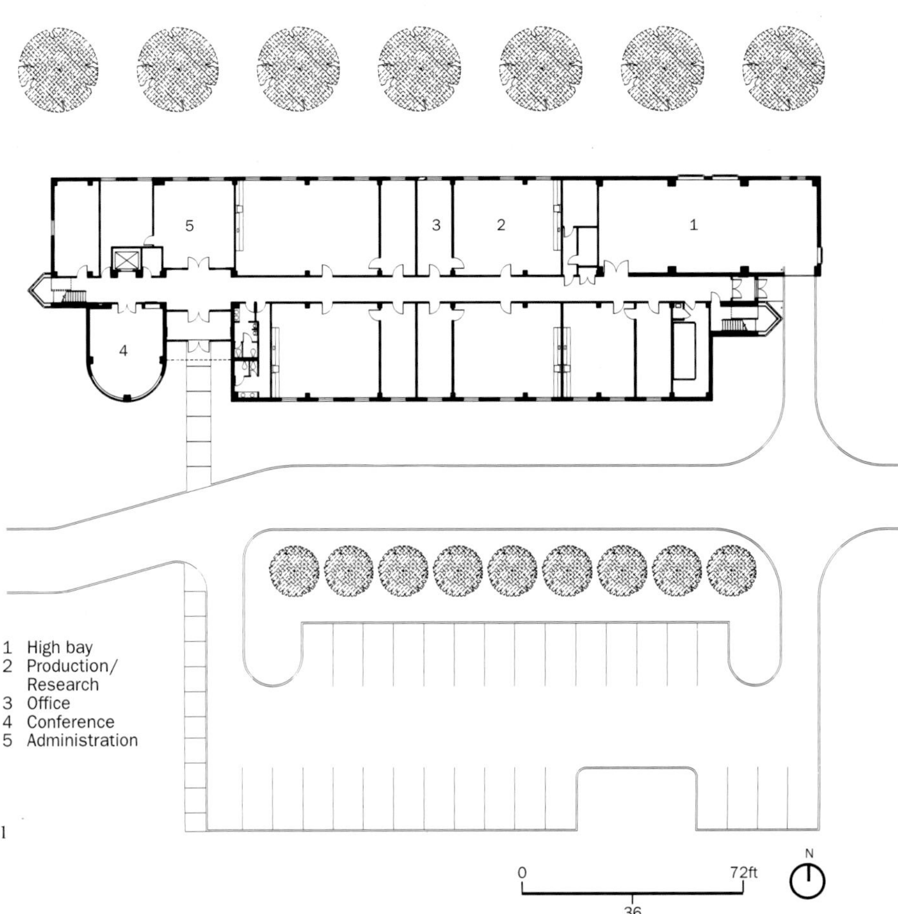

1

2

3

4

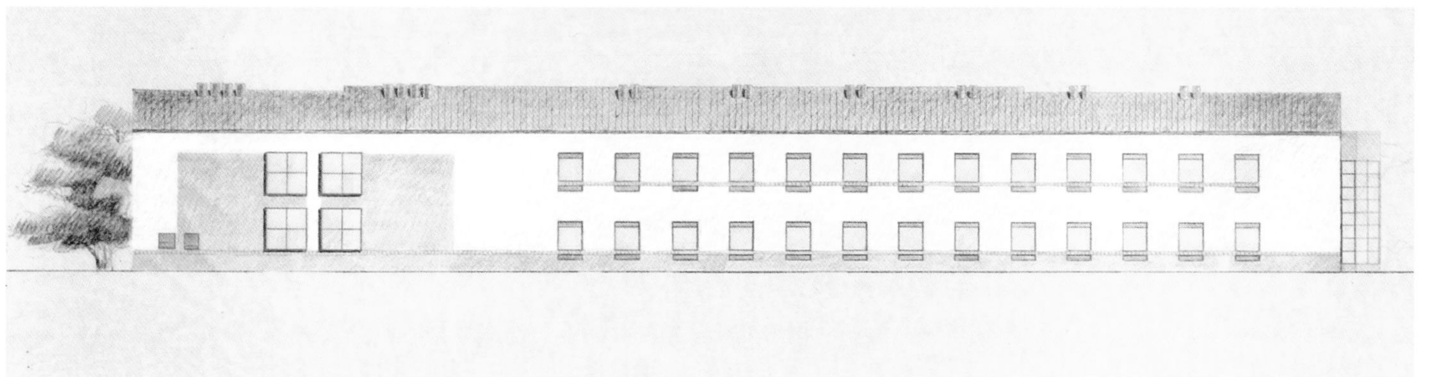

5

1 Ground-floor plan
2 View from the north-east
3&4 South elevation
5 North elevation

6

7

6 Conference room
7 West stair tower
8 Central corridor looking west
9 West stair
10 High bay

8

9

10

Stafford Hall, Microbiology/Orthopaedics Research Building

Design/Completion 1990/1993
Burlington, Vermont
The University of Vermont
75,000 square feet
Molded red brick, limestone accents, metal roof

As part of a development master plan, expanded research laboratories for the Microbiology Department and muscular-skeletal clinical research laboratories are provided on this medical school campus. Careful site planning provides two new important spaces: a garden study court and a campus quadrangle whose approach axis is terminated by the building's articulated fourth floor conference room.

On the first floor, a gallery overlooking the courtyard and quadrangle connects multiple entrances and adjoining buildings. The second and third floors contain perimeter research laboratories and offices, and centralized support facilities; the fourth floor houses clinical laboratories and offices for muscular-skeletal researchers.

Research laboratories organized on a 10' x 32' module promote the development of an efficient organization of benchwork, fumehoods and services, and provides flexibility for future alterations.

"To complement its 19th century neighbors, the building is composed in formal tripartite parti, with a pitched roof and fluted brick louvers at the gable ends."
Jan Keane, FAIA

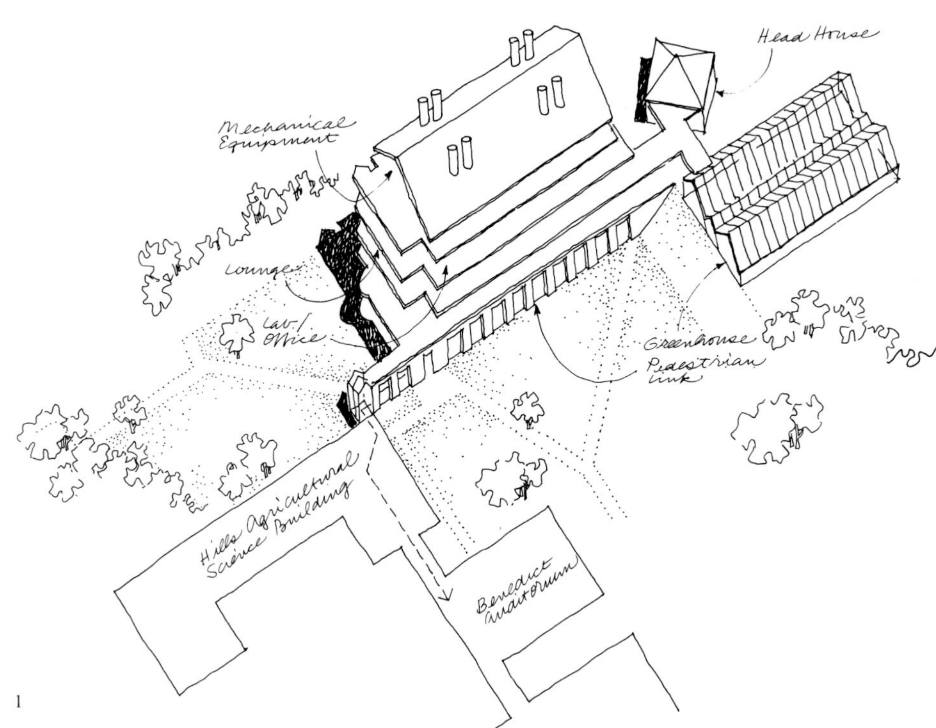

1

1 Sketched site plan
2 View of north facade
3 View of greenhouses looking north-east

2

3

4

5

6

7

8

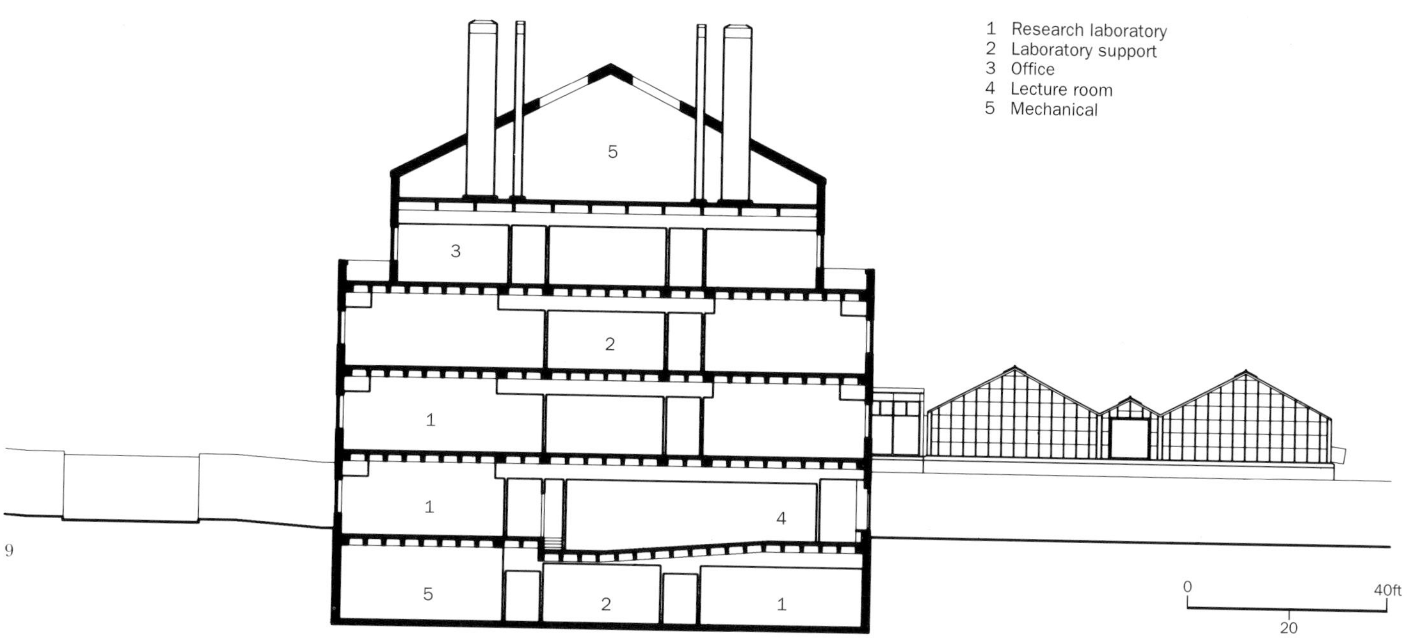

9

4 Detail of north facade
5 Stair detail of north facade
6 View of north facade
7 View of west facade
8 Stair detail of south facade
9 Section

10 First-floor plan
11 Fourth-floor plan
12 Lobby tile mural
13 Laboratory corridor
14 First floor gallery
15 Upper level of lounge

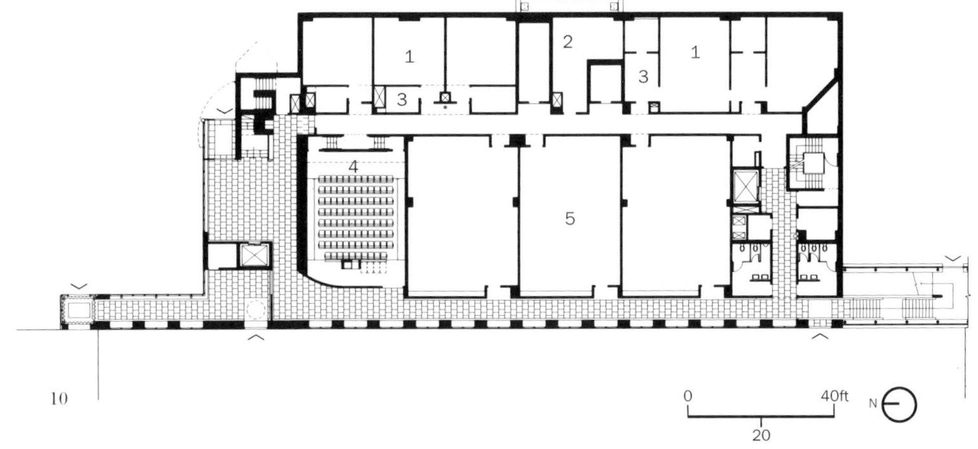

10

1 Research laboratory
2 Laboratory support
3 Office
4 Lecture room
5 Teaching laboratory
6 Student workroom
7 Classroom

11

12

13

14

15

16

17

16 Corridor view
17 Lecture room
18 Teaching laboratory
19 Research laboratory

18

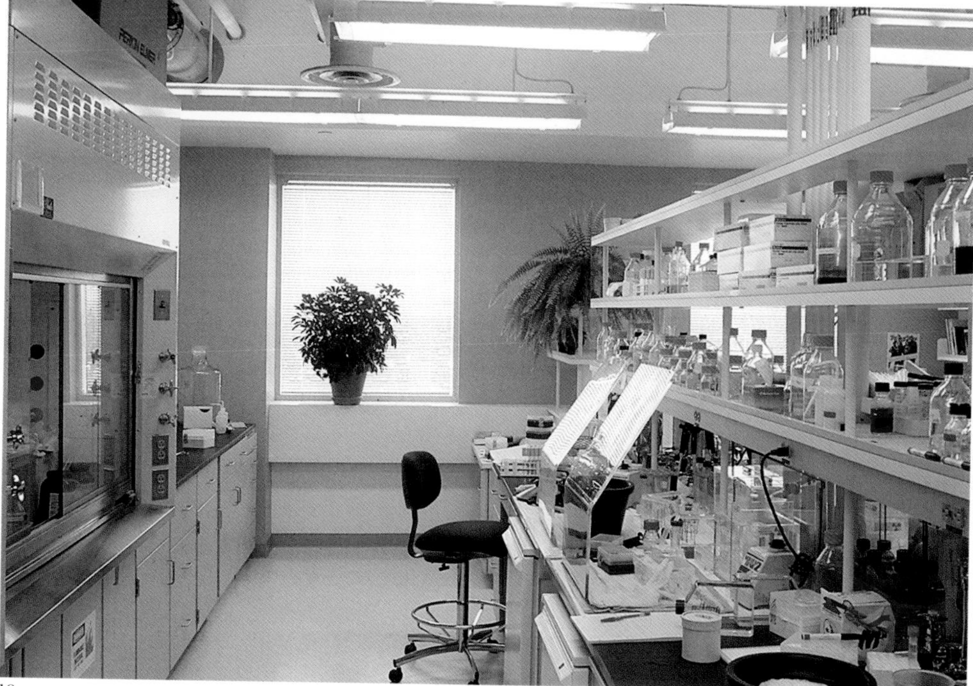
19

Laboratory Science Building

Design/Completion 1992/1995
Staten Island, New York
College of Staten Island, The City University of New York
121,000 square feet
Hand-molded brick, cast stone accents, glass curtain wall, metal windows

The new science laboratory building combines biology, chemistry, environmental science and neuroscience research and teaching facilities. The structure is a prototype for future buildings that will fill in the open corners of two existing campus quadrangles.

Classrooms and labs are wrapped around a courtyard, providing the possibility for synergy between the two activities. A hierarchy of spaces leads visitors from the campus quadrangle to the courtyard and finally into the shared spaces of the building. The wings are connected at the first and third levels; the ground level is open to allow free passage between the parking lot and the campus.

A repetitive building module facilitates a systematic organization of the program and at the same time allows flexibility for future change. The concrete structure and relatively short spans help to minimize vibration, thus creating an ideal environment for the use of highly sensitive equipment.

"The visible expression of the greenhouse on the curved corner of the building sets the building apart from its neighbors and celebrates the activities within."
Paul Broches, FAIA

1

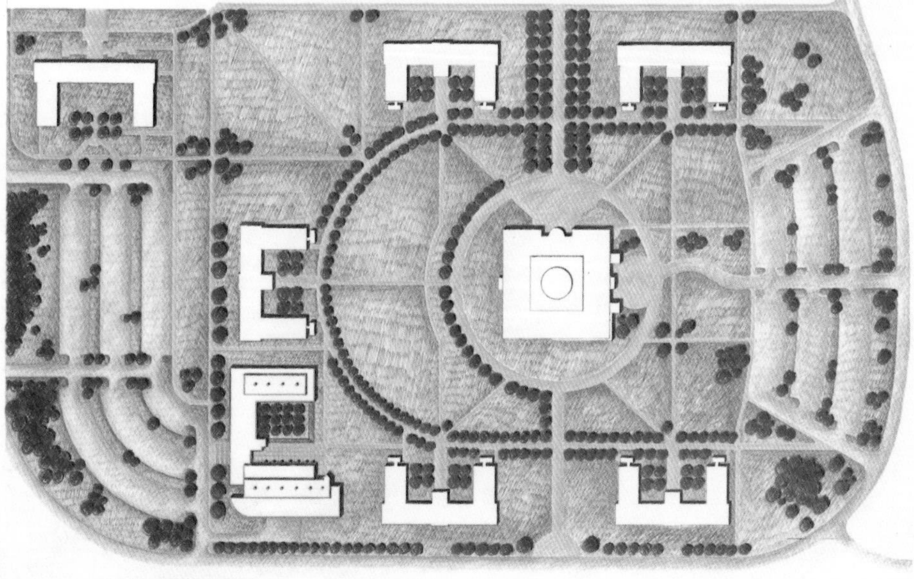

2

1 Courtyard stair
2 Campus plan, south quadrangle
3 Entry from parking
4 West elevation

3

4

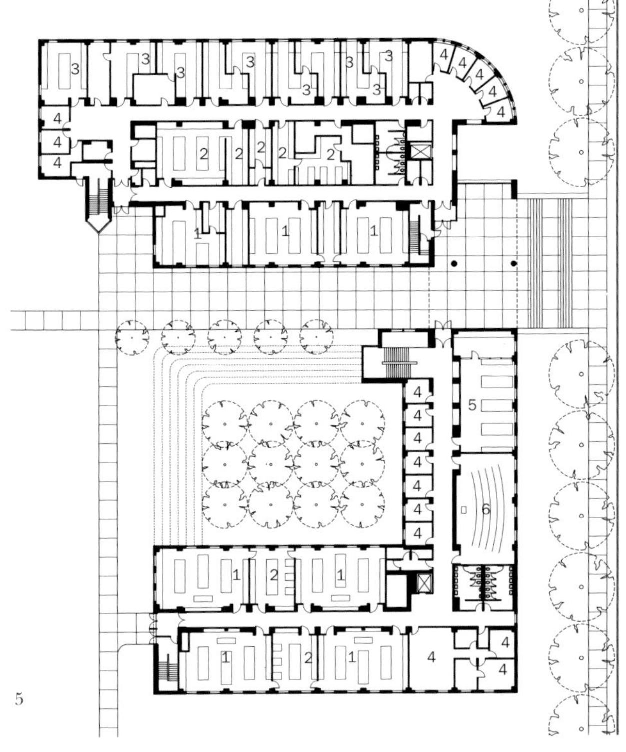

5

1 Teaching laboratory
2 Laboratory support
3 Research laboratory
4 Office
5 Computer laboratory
6 Lecture hall

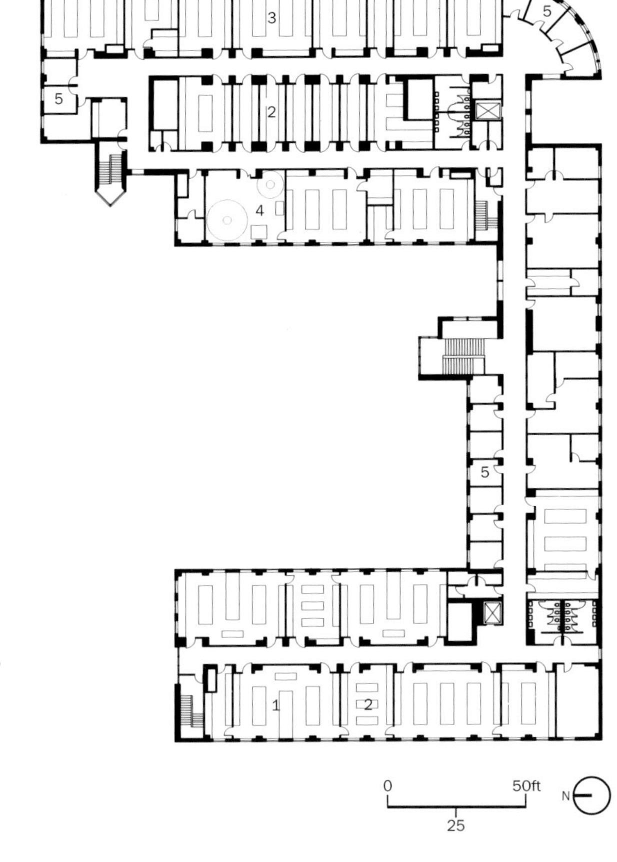

6

7

5 First-floor plan
6 Second-floor plan
7 Sketch of south-west corner
8 Typical laboratory
9 Central stair with mural by Valerie Jaudon
10 West elevation

8

9

10

Metcalfe Student Center

Design/Completion 1993/1995
Brooklyn, New York
Long Island University, Brooklyn Campus
27,650 square feet
Brick and terra cotta exterior, marble, carved plaster, terrazzo interior finishes

The Metcalfe Building, formerly the Paramount Movie Theater, is the main administrative and academic building on the LIU Brooklyn Campus. Renovations to the exterior, basement, and first three floors, together with the construction of the adjacent new Health Sciences Center, create a vibrant new center to the campus.

The original three-story vaulted movie theater lobby, the Great Hall, has been converted for use as a cafeteria and grand ceremonial space. Monumental new lighting fixtures in the Great Hall cast a warm glow throughout the public spaces, while a new air conditioning system woven carefully into the existing ceilings tempers the air. Student government and student clubs are located prominently on the mezzanine overlooking the Great Hall.

A new canopy and sign which recall the original Paramount Theater are planned. Together these improvements create a strong new identity for this growing downtown campus.

"Restoration of the former vaudeville marble and carved plaster lobby creates a much needed amenity and a central gathering place for this commuter school." Paul Broches, FAIA

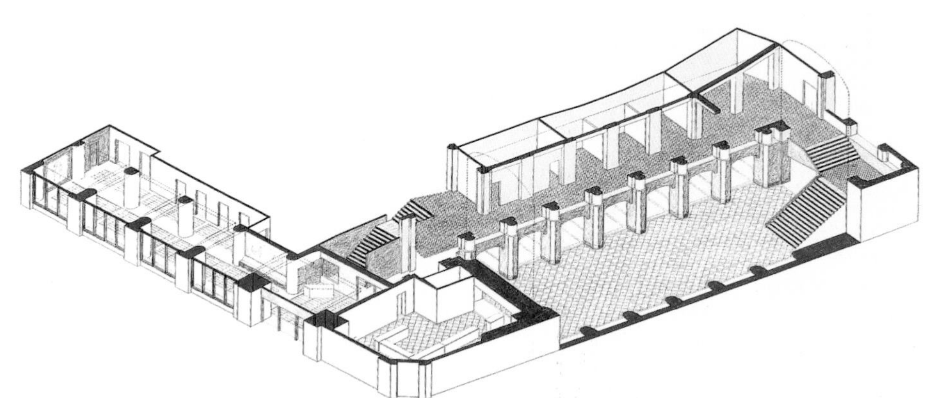

1

2

1 Isometric of public areas
2 Meeting area
3 The Great Hall

3

Zeckendorf Health Sciences Center

Design/Completion 1993/1995
Brooklyn, New York
Long Island University, Brooklyn Campus
103,000 square feet
Steel frame with brick exterior, cast stone and metal panel accents

The Health Sciences Center provides new classrooms, laboratories, faculty offices, and administrative space for the College of Pharmacy and Health Sciences, and the College of Nursing of Long Island University. In addition, several large lecture rooms for use by the entire university are located in the building. The corner site serves as a major pedestrian and vehicular entrance to the campus. The new building, a southern gateway to the campus, is flanked by a new gate and guard kiosk. Included in the program are six stories of programmed space, a rooftop penthouse, and a partial basement which contains mechanical systems.

University lecture rooms are located on the first floor, with the building lobby, primary entrance, and elevators at the north, facing the courtyard. Administrative areas on the upper floors overlook the courtyard. Faculty offices are arranged along the west side of the building facing the pedestrian corridor.

"The clock tower marks an important gateway into the campus, and at the same time, its chimes project the University's presence into the surrounding downtown."
John Kurtz, AIA

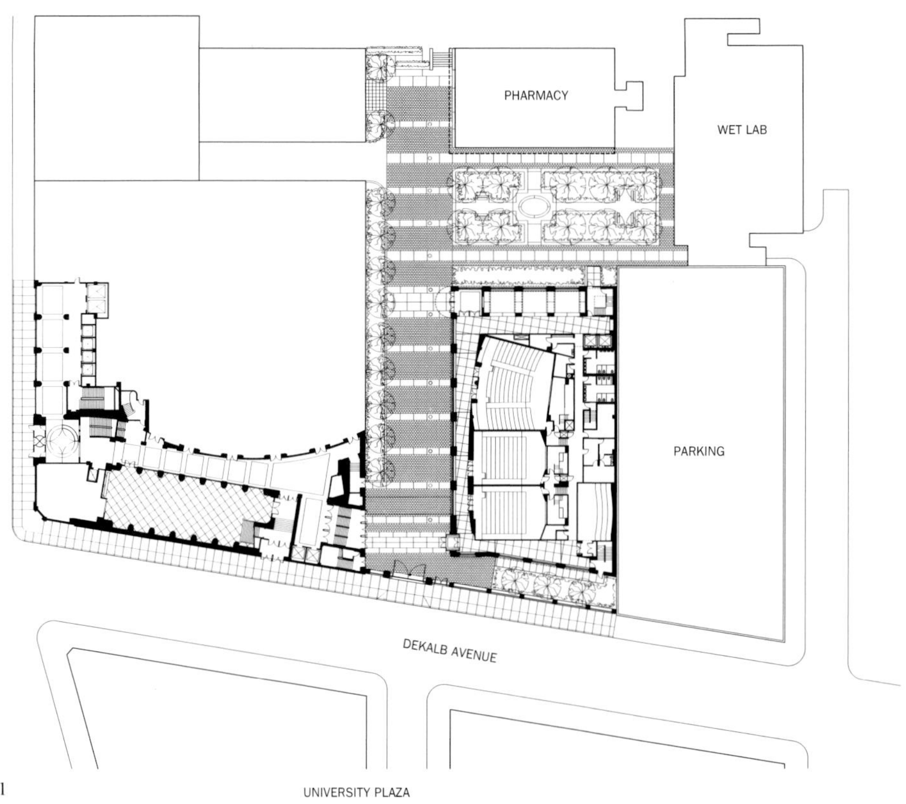

1

2

1 Site plan
2 Looking east on DeKalb Avenue
3 Looking north on pedestrian street

3

4

5

6

4 Clock tower lounge
5 Corridor to lecture hall
6 Lecture hall
7 Looking south on pedestrian street
8 Detail of clock tower
9 Bridge to new student center

7

8

9

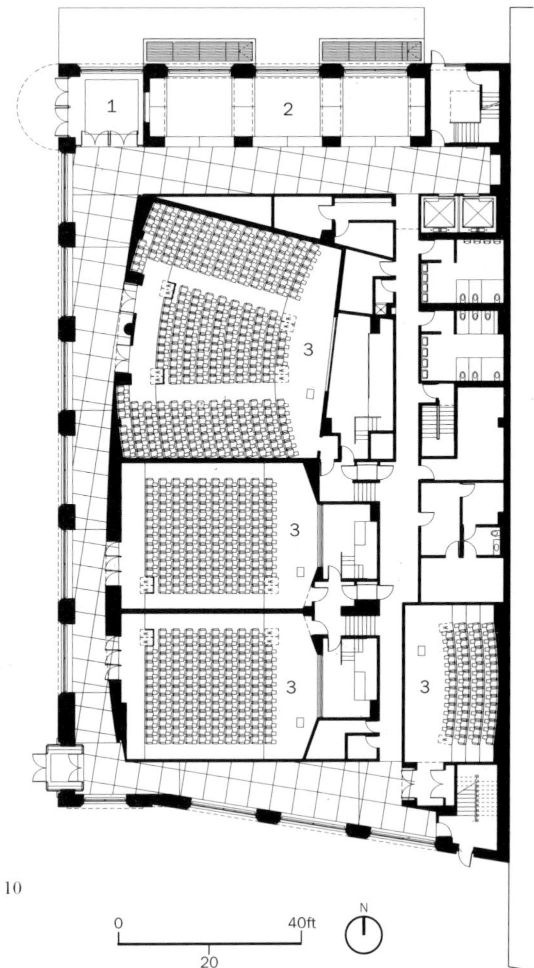

10

1 Entry
2 Lounge
3 Lecture hall

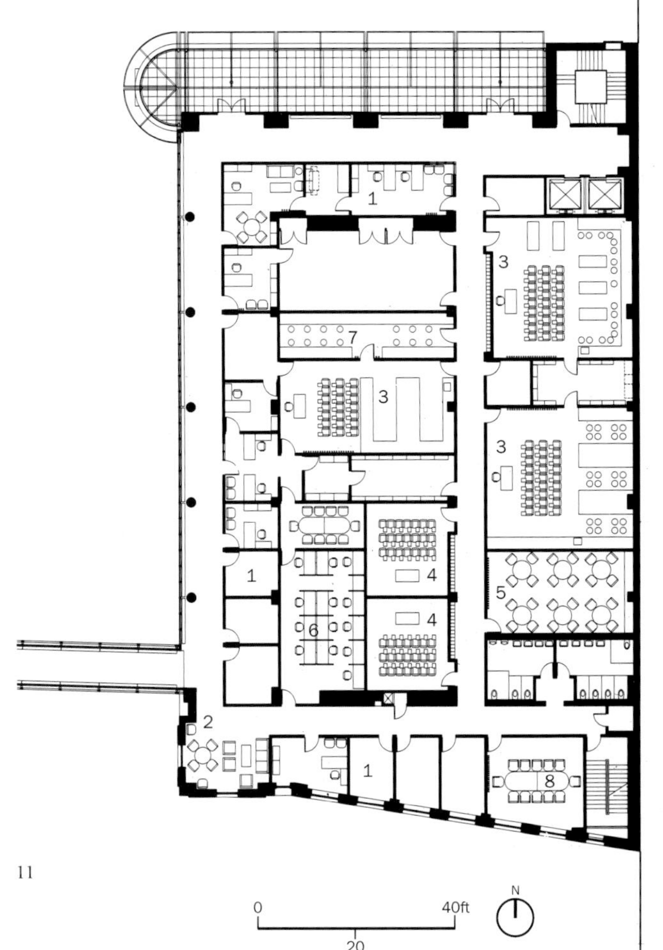

11

1 Faculty office
2 Lounge
3 Teaching laboratory
4 Classroom
5 Study center
6 Adjunct faculty
7 Computer laboratory
8 Conference room

12

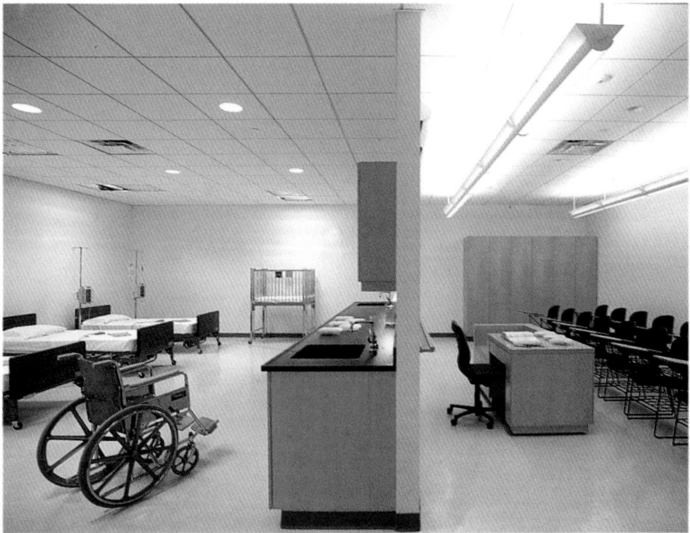

13

10 Ground-floor plan
11 Third-floor plan
12 Teaching laboratory
13 Demonstration laboratory
14 Student lounge
15 Clock window
16 Student lounge

14

15

16

Administrative and Student Services Building

Design/Completion 1993/1997
Bronx, New York
Hostos Community College, The City University of New York
170,000 square feet
Aluminum and glass curtain wall, brick exterior, glazed block and glass partitions, terrazzo floors

Hostos Community College is the fastest growing campus in the City of New York system. To accommodate this growth, the original 1960s office building will be completely renovated. The work includes total replacement of the exterior facade, interior demolition, asbestos abatement, new mechanical and electrical infrastructure, and the addition of two floors to the building. The solution features a considerably lighter and more economical cladding to create a state-of-the-art curtain wall.

The expanded facility accommodates the administration, student services, departmental offices, classrooms, a television studio, and large lecture rooms. It contains state-of-the-art telecommunications/data services, including a computer information center, a multi-link training laboratory, and an on-line advanced technology interactive teaching classroom with rear projection.

"To bridge the busy Grand Concourse and make a visible focus on the campus, we chose light colored metal panels and an extensive amount of glass to communicate openness and accessibility."
Paul Broches, FAIA

1

2

1 Existing office building
2 West elevation
3 Overall campus view from south-west
4&5 Detail of exterior building

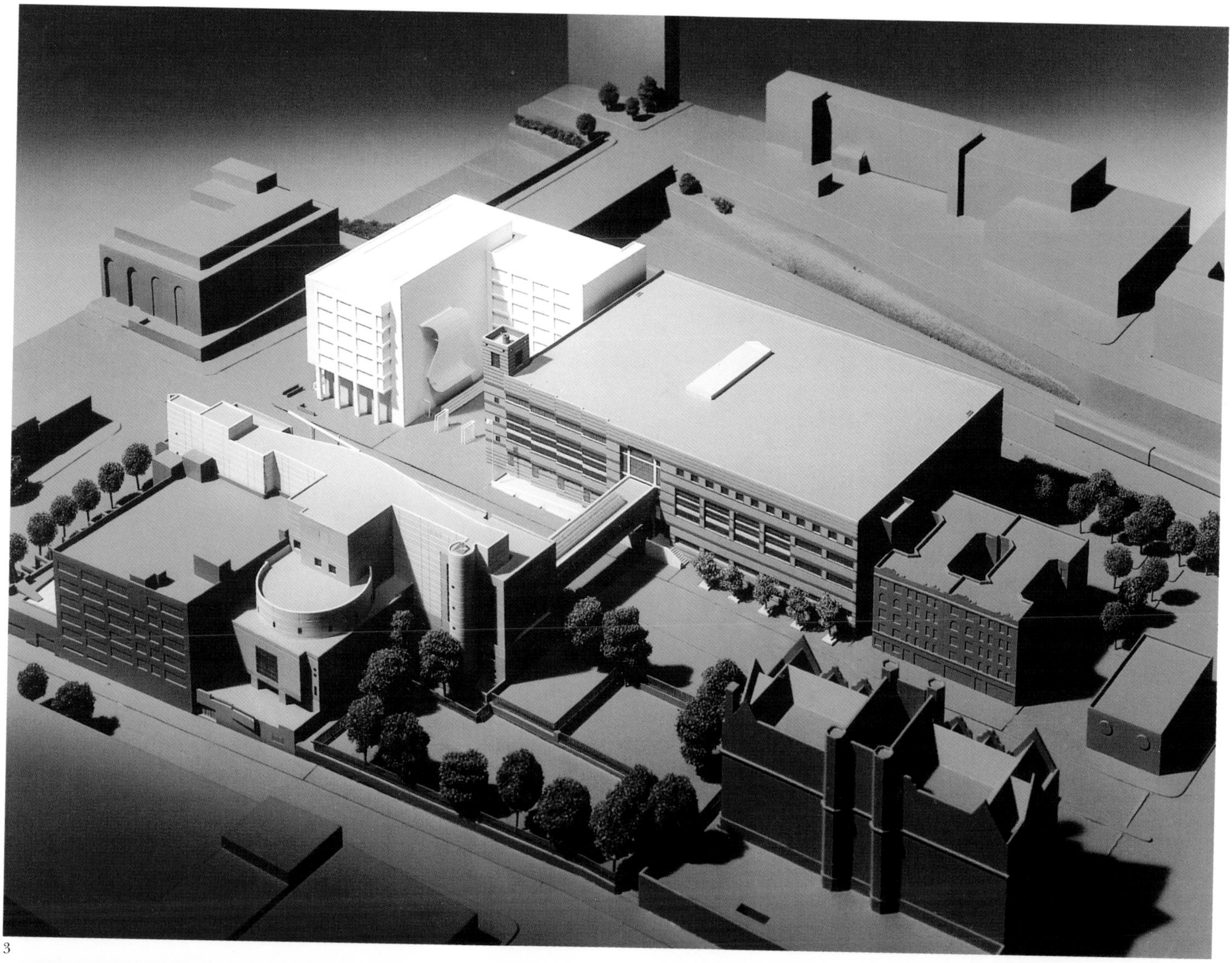

3

4

5

PS 88, The Seneca School

Design/Completion 1994/1996
Queens, New York
New York City School Construction Authority
60,608 square feet renovation
47,561 square feet addition
Steel frame with molded red brick, terra cotta accents, painted aluminum windows, glazed block walls and terrazzo floors

Originally built in 1907, this five-story neo-classical structure is the chief landmark in a residential neighborhood of two- and three-story row houses.

Two-story additions have been added to the ends of the existing building to nearly double the area of the school and, at the same time, to reduce its apparent size. New stair and elevator towers replace outmoded and non-complying stairs. The west wing houses a new boiler plant and gym; the east wing houses 19 classrooms. Modernization of the existing building includes a 400-seat lunchroom, a kitchen, and upgrading of mechanical, electrical and data systems.

On the exterior, the two new wings form a welcoming entry court and reinforce the symmetry of the original neo-classical building. Brick, terra cotta and stone details and projecting bays have been introduced to integrate with the historical qualities of the original structure.

"The introduction of two new entries at ground level replaces the daunting stairs of the original building. A playful use of terra cotta and the integration of children's art animate the interior."
Paul Broches, FAIA

1 Gym
2 Auditorium
3 Classroom
4 Kindergarten
5 Administration
6 Mechanical

1

0 20 40ft
N

2

1 First-floor plan
2 Detail of front elevation
3 Existing south elevation
4&5 South elevation

3

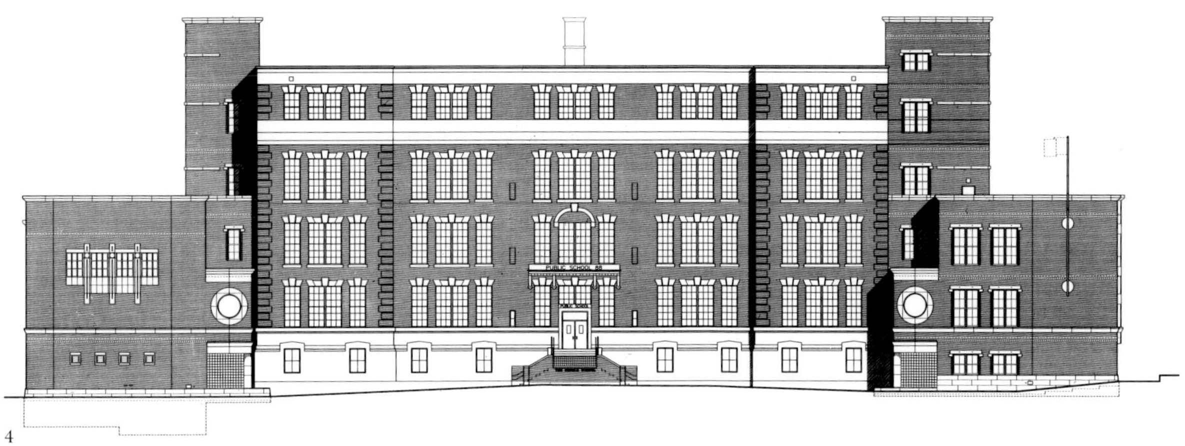

4

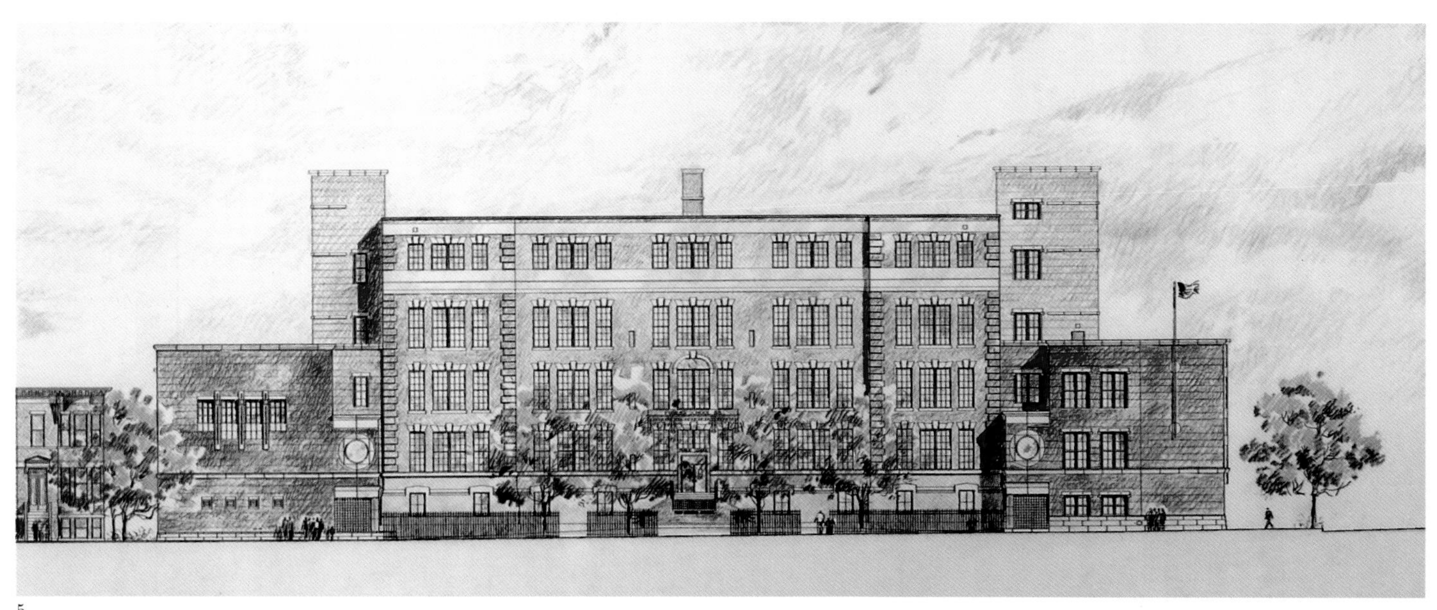

5

PS 56, Richmond Elementary School

Design/Completion 1994/1997
Staten Island, New York
New York City School Construction Authority
Associate architect: Roberta Washington Architect, PC
98,000 square feet
Steel frame with red and buff brick exterior, metal panels, painted aluminum windows, standing seam metal roof

This new elementary school is located in a residential area consisting of single- and dual-family dwellings built in the past ten years. As the only civic structure in the neighborhood, it has great significance in the community. Accommodating administrative offices, a gymnasium, a cafeteria, and a 450-seat auditorium, the school provides a location for recreation leagues, town meetings, and other after-hours uses.

The site slopes from a high point at the intersection of two streets to a low point at the opposite corner. Taking advantage of the slope of the site, the school is three stories high on the south side facing the adjacent residential development and four stories on the playground side. The building is located on the north side of the site to allow the playground to benefit from southern sunlight.

"By articulating individual program elements and introducing pattern and two colors of brick to the facade, we tried to give the building both a civic scale for the community and an intimate scale for its young users." John Kurtz, AIA

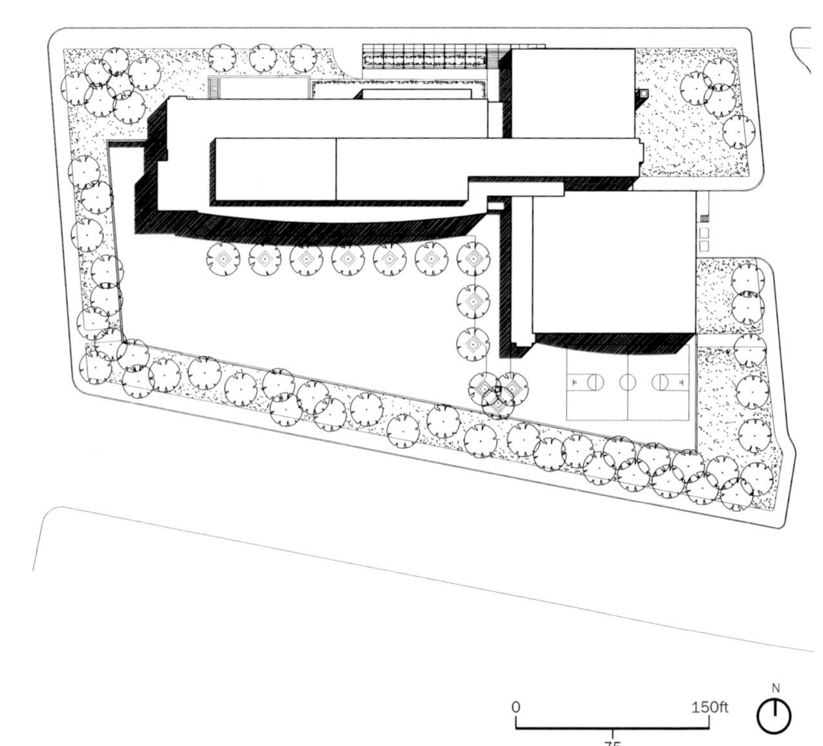

1

2

1 Site plan
2 South elevation
3 East elevation
4 North elevation

3

4

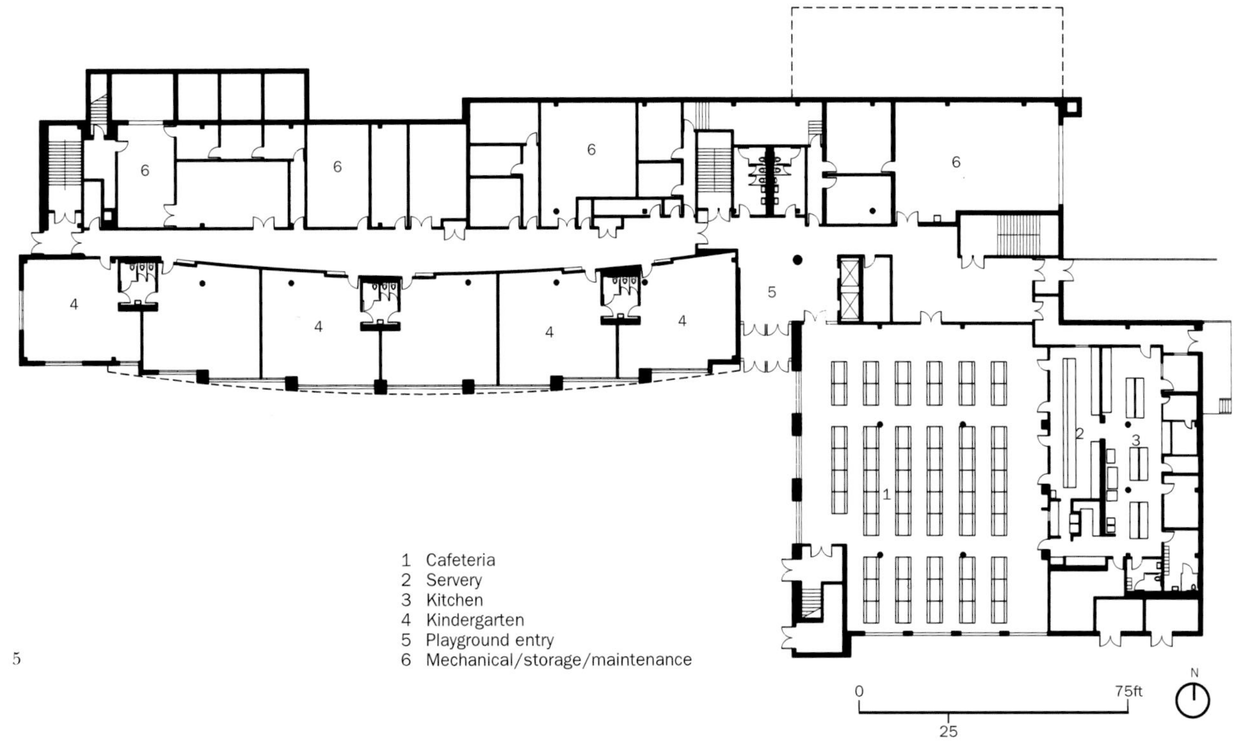
1 Cafeteria
2 Servery
3 Kitchen
4 Kindergarten
5 Playground entry
6 Mechanical/storage/maintenance
0
25
75ft
N

5

6

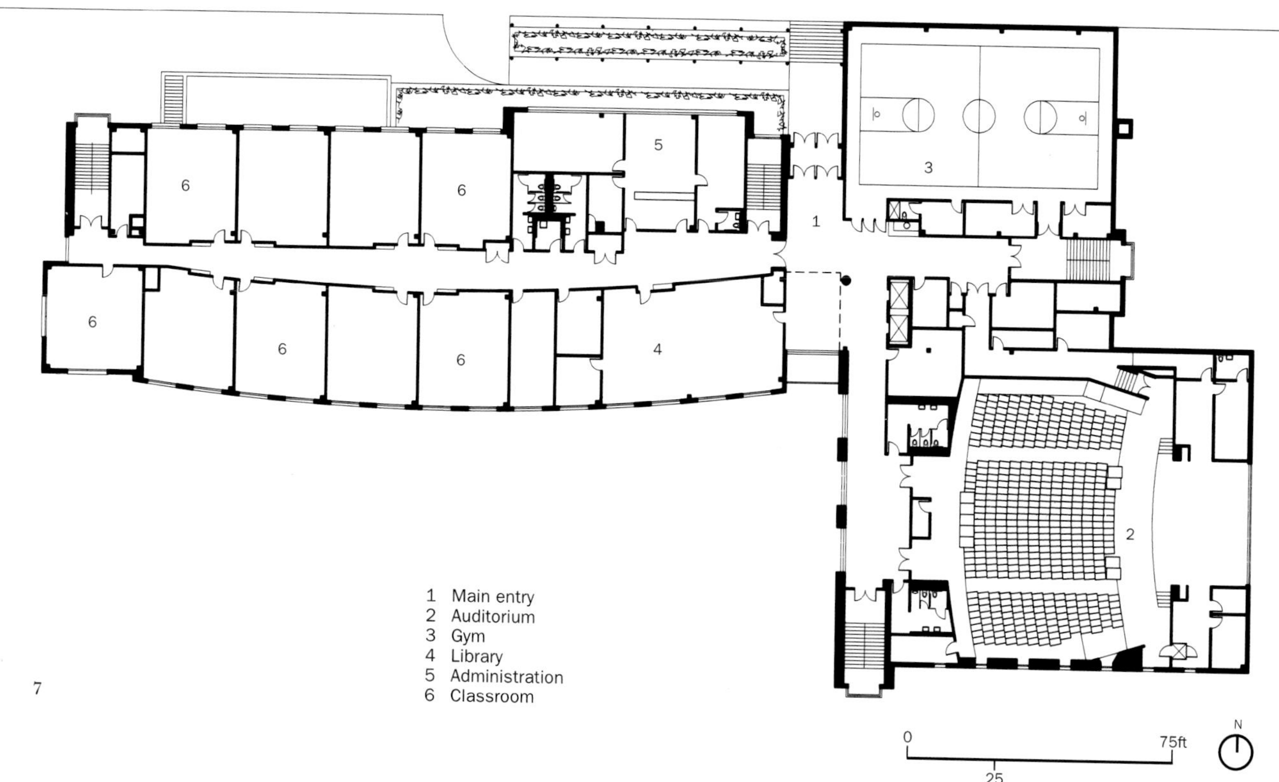

7

8

5 First-floor plan
6 South elevation detail
7 Lower level plan
8 Main corridor with classroom display cabinets

WORK PLACES

Volvo Corporate Headquarters

Design/Completion 1982/1985
Gothenburg, Sweden
AB Volvo
Associate architect: Owe Svard
106,000 square feet
Cast-in-place concrete frame with precast concrete panels and granite corner insets
Teak, green marble, porcelain tiles, brass fixtures

Reflecting a new organizational structure as a result of a merger, the new headquarters for AB Volvo represents the value of human industry and craftsmanship embodied by the expanded Volvo companies.

The building form is determined by three major functional elements and the rugged nature of its hilltop site. The building is approached by a winding roadway which terminates in an elongated formal entry circle reminiscent of the traditional Swedish farm court. A free-standing curved wall of dark green marble defines the main entrance at the mid-level of the stepped three-story structure.

Once inside the entrance, one looks onto a formal cloister-like courtyard, formed by conference and executive offices on two sides and an arcade and gallery on the other two sides. The gallery continues the full width of the building and forms the main circulation between the reception area to the south, a three-level corporate wing to the west, the executive quarters to the north, and the visitors area to the east.

"The villa-like setting offers places of contemplation and reflection in marked contrast to the high-pressure corporate world." Mark Markiewicz, AIA

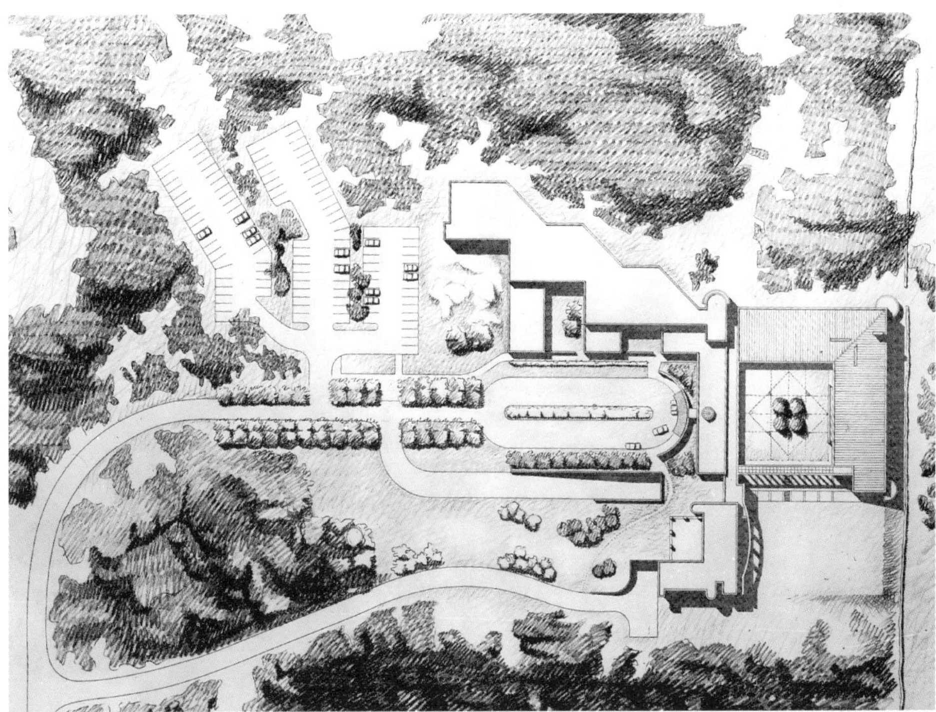

1

2

1 Site plan
2 Entry forecourt
3 Schematic site plan
4 View from the west

3

4

5 South elevation
6 North elevation
7 South elevation with visitors' wing
8 East–west section looking south
9 Aerial view with assembly plant beyond
10 North elevation of visitors' wing

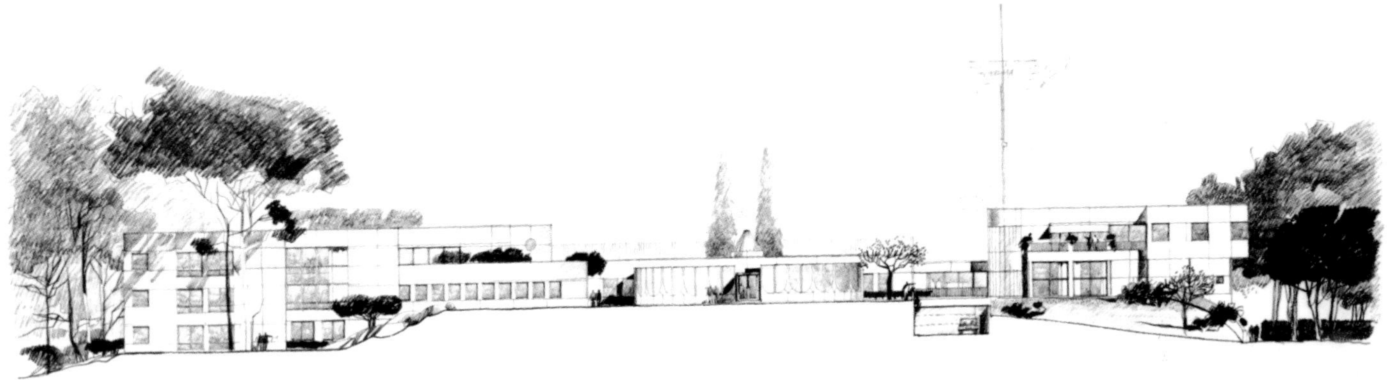

5

6

7

8

9

10

11 Entry-floor plan
12 View from the north-east
13 Corporate wing
14 Executive wing

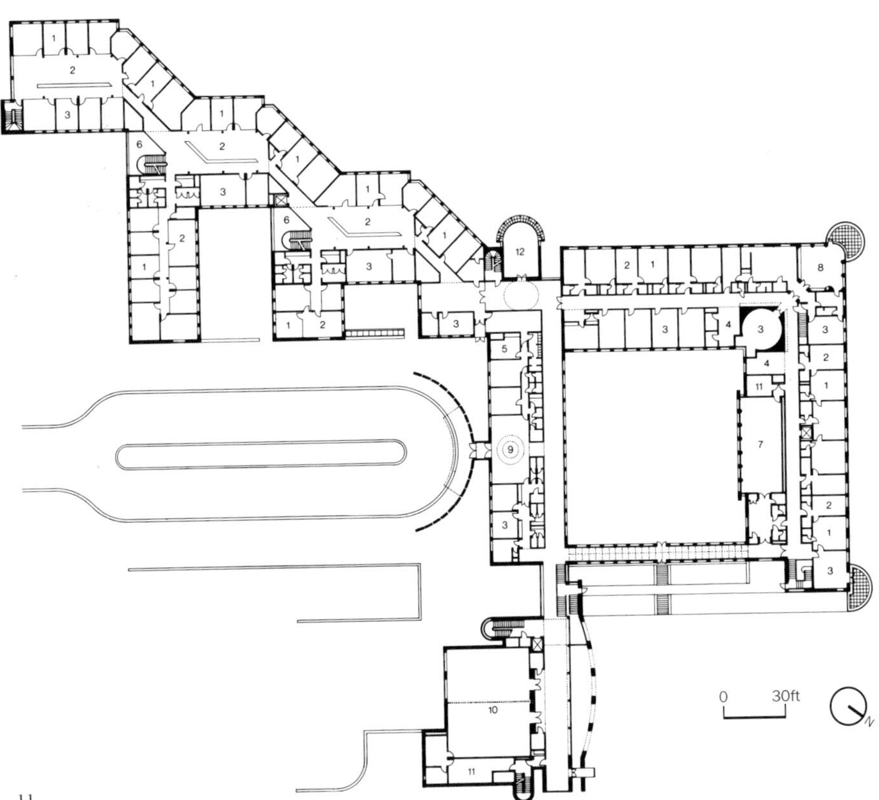

11

1 Office
2 Secretary
3 Conference room
4 Lounge
5 Services
6 Open to below
7 Boardroom
8 President's office
9 Reception
10 Auditorium
11 Projection room
12 Library

12

13

14

15

16

15 Main entry gallery with stair to staff dining room
16 Main entry lobby
17 Atrium in corporate wing
18 Corridor in executive wing
19 Entry gallery with porcelain mural by Lin Utzon

17

18

19

20

21

22

20 Boardroom with tapestry by Lin Utzon
21 Multipurpose conference room
22 Entry gallery at conference room
23 Staff dining room

23

24&26 Library
25 Chairman's office
27 Stair to executive dining room with mural by Jennifer Bartlett

24

25

26

27

28

29

30

28 Executive conference room
29 North arcade
30 Open workstations in corporate wing
31 Daily conference room

31

300 Atlantic Street Office Building

Design/Completion 1983/1990
Stamford, Connecticut
F.D. Rich Company
257,000 square feet office
295,000 square feet parking
Precast concrete, limestone panels with granite accents

Located in downtown Stamford at the first major intersection north of Interstate 95, this complex consists of ground level retail space, a double-story arcade, and 12 office floors. An adjacent parking garage contains four levels above grade and two levels below grade. A pedestrian bridge connects office and parking above a landscaped courtyard.

A gently curving facade acknowledges the building's presence as a "gateway" to the central business district. The curved facade is accentuated by a vertical notch which marks the building entry, anchors the building to the intersection of two major roadways, allows light to enter each elevator lobby above grade, and provides views to the Long Island Sound.

The building steps down in height to respond to the smaller scale of adjacent buildings along Atlantic Street. The office tower facade is precast concrete spandrel beams clad in white Italian Apricena limestone panels with an accent strip of Verde Mergozzo granite.

"The L-shaped plan and curved streetwall provide an entry plaza for the public and a series of interior garden courtyards for the building occupants."
Steven M. Goldberg, FAIA

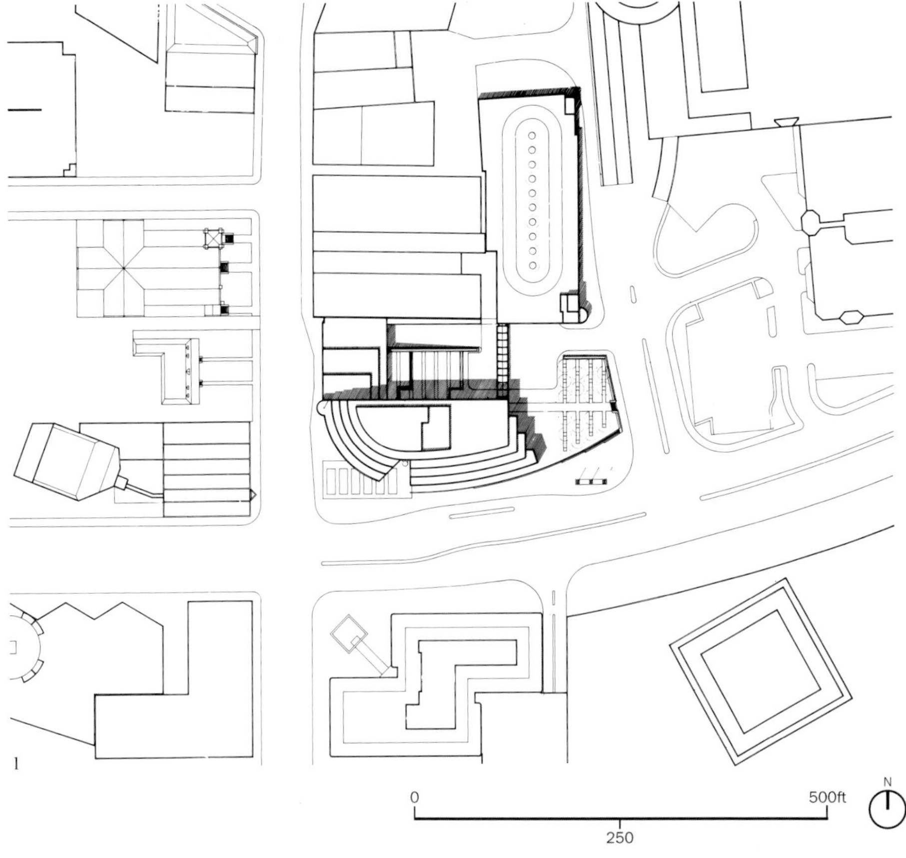

1

2

1 Site plan
2 View from the west
3 View toward plaza and interior courtyards
4 Street view

3

4

5 Office entry portico
6 Lobby gallery

5

6

7 Mezzanine
8 Street level lobby
9 Elevator lobby at ground-floor
10 Bridge to parking garage

7

8

9

10

Center West, Office/Retail/Parking

Design/Completion 1984/1990
Los Angeles, California
Center West
Associate architect: Daniel, Mann, Johnson & Mendenhall
290,000 square feet office
24,000 square feet retail
290,000 square feet parking
Steel frame with exterior cladding of red Karelia granite in thermal and polished finishes; painted aluminum curtain wall

This office building bridges two scales of urbanity characteristic of a fast-growing metropolis: high-density development on the edge of a treasured pedestrian-scale village unique to Los Angeles. The complex reinforces the grandeur of Wilshire Boulevard and at the same time engages the intimacy of the adjoining village of Westwood.

The south facade facing Wilshire Boulevard steps away from the building mass and stands independently as a symbolic sentinel. Its deepset windows shade the glass and visually strengthen the wall. Clear heat-absorbing glass has been utilized to enhance the transparency of the "punched" windows in the exterior wall, and to contrast with the wall mass. The granite cladding has a warm rose cast and rough texture. Vertical glazed slices through the building articulate the mass, reinforcing its verticality, and help to reduce the scale of the tower to effect the transition from civic boulevard to village street.

"The first experience of the building for the occupants entering by car is a multi-level light-filled room that provides a visual connection to the active street and upper level lobby." Steven M. Goldberg, FAIA

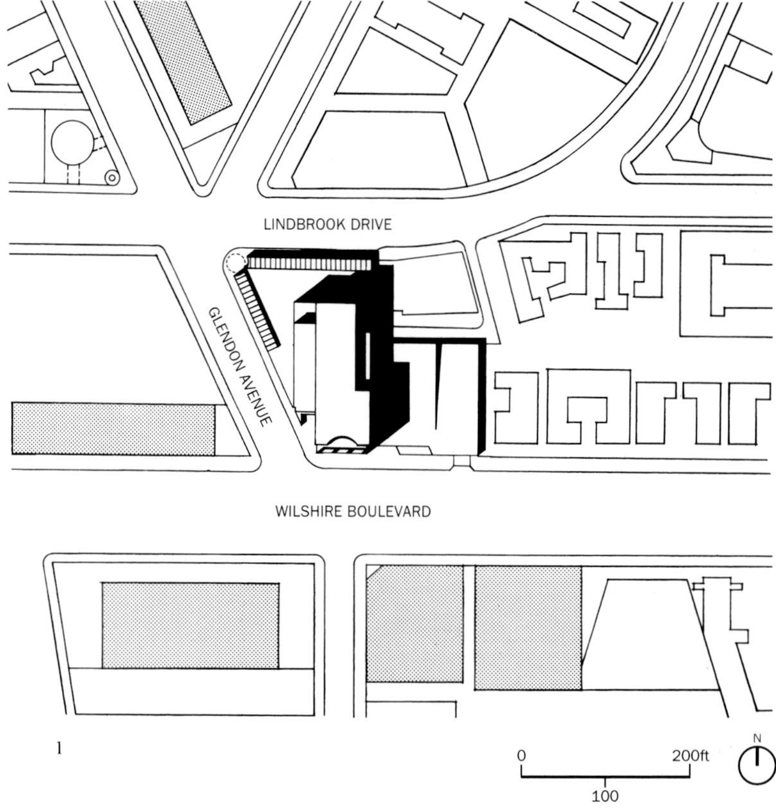

1

2

1 Site plan
2 South elevation
3 View from the north-west

3

4 Trellis at north-west entry to retail
5 Facade detail

4

5

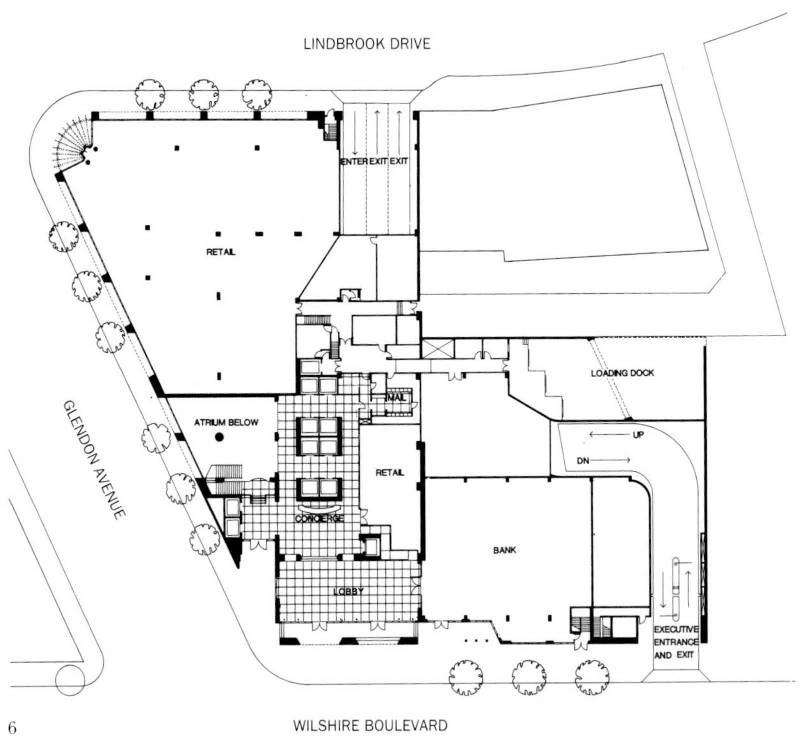

LINDBROOK DRIVE
ENTER EXIT EXIT
RETAIL
LOADING DOCK
GLENDON AVENUE
ATRIUM BELOW
MAIL
RETAIL
UP
DN
CONCIERGE
BANK
LOBBY
EXECUTIVE ENTRANCE AND EXIT
WILSHIRE BOULEVARD

6

McCORMICK

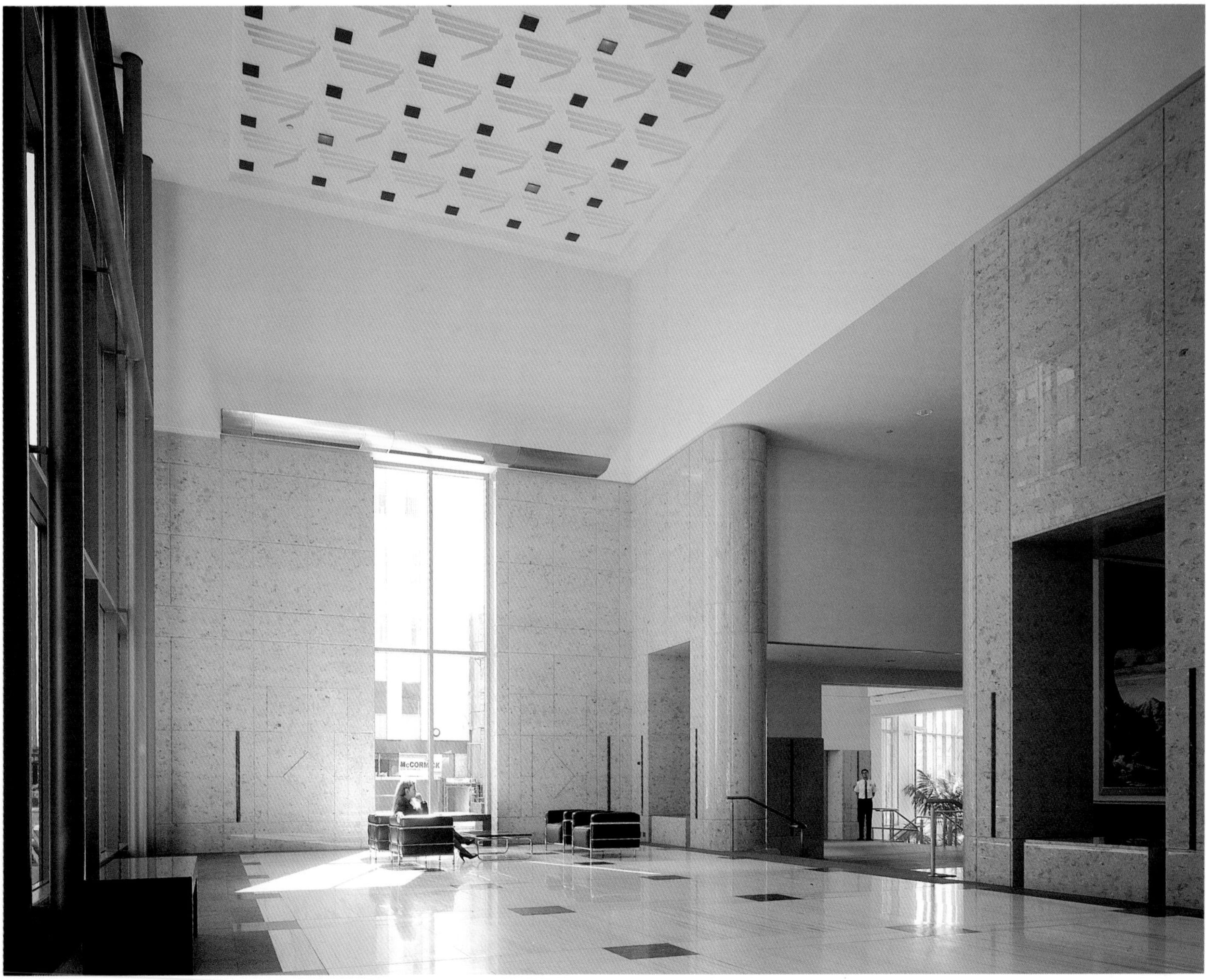

7

6 Site plan/ground floor
7 Main lobby
8 Wilshire Boulevard lobby
9 Lobby area

8

9

10 Stair to lower level lobby
11 Atrium lobby at lower parking level

10

11

Solana Office/Parking Complex

Design/Completion 1986/1989
Westlake/Southlake, Texas
IBM Corporation/Maguire Thomas Partners
1,730,000 square feet
Precast concrete, stucco plaster facades, limestone, concrete, granite, insulating glass, aluminum frames

Solana is a mixed-use complex which, when complete, will include 6 million square feet of office space, a 400-room hotel, and retail shopping and recreational facilities for over 10,000 people. The master plan phase created a site plan which preserves the character of the 840-acre south-western site and developed design guidelines and an architectural language for all buildings.

The low-rise campus in phase one includes six office buildings, a computer building, a dining pavilion, and parking. The widely dispersed sites for 400,000- to 600,000-square foot buildings are organized along a stream and road, culminating in a symbolic and actual community center. The office buildings are linked by landscaped pedestrian streets and a winding waterway which flows through the village center. Two L-shaped parking garages frame the entry approach to the center of the complex and establish a strong urban core.

"Deep stucco walls define the built limits of each precinct within the rolling prairie landscape."
Jan Keane, FAIA

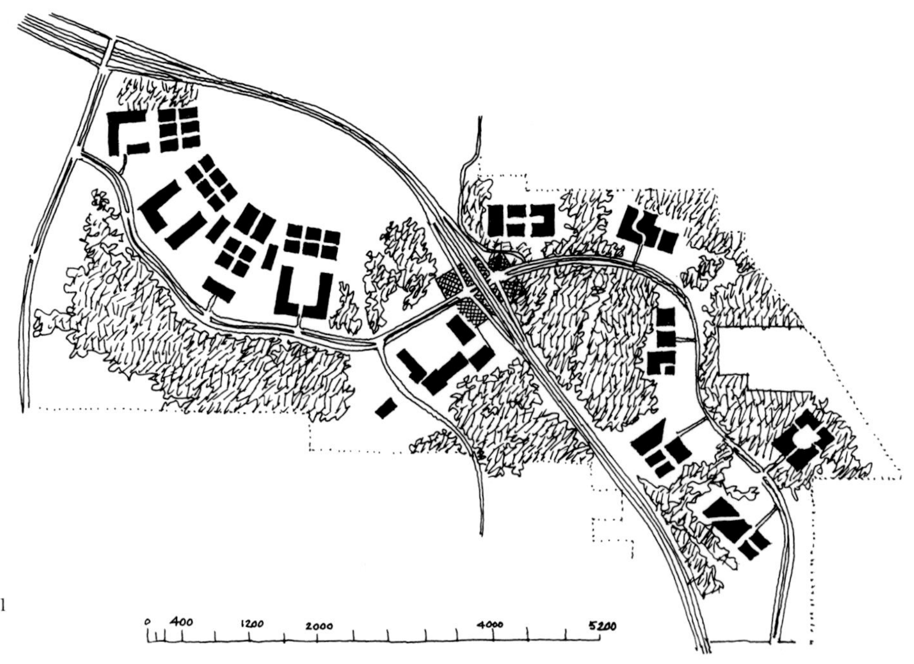

1

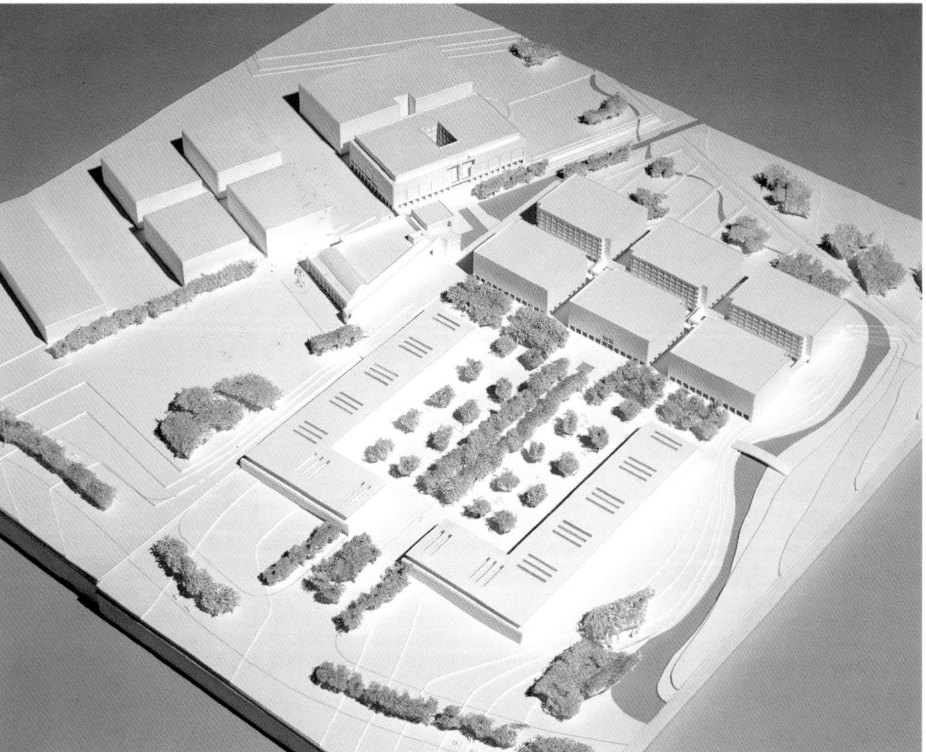

2

1 Master plan
2 Model of master plan complex
3 Central pedestrian street

3

4

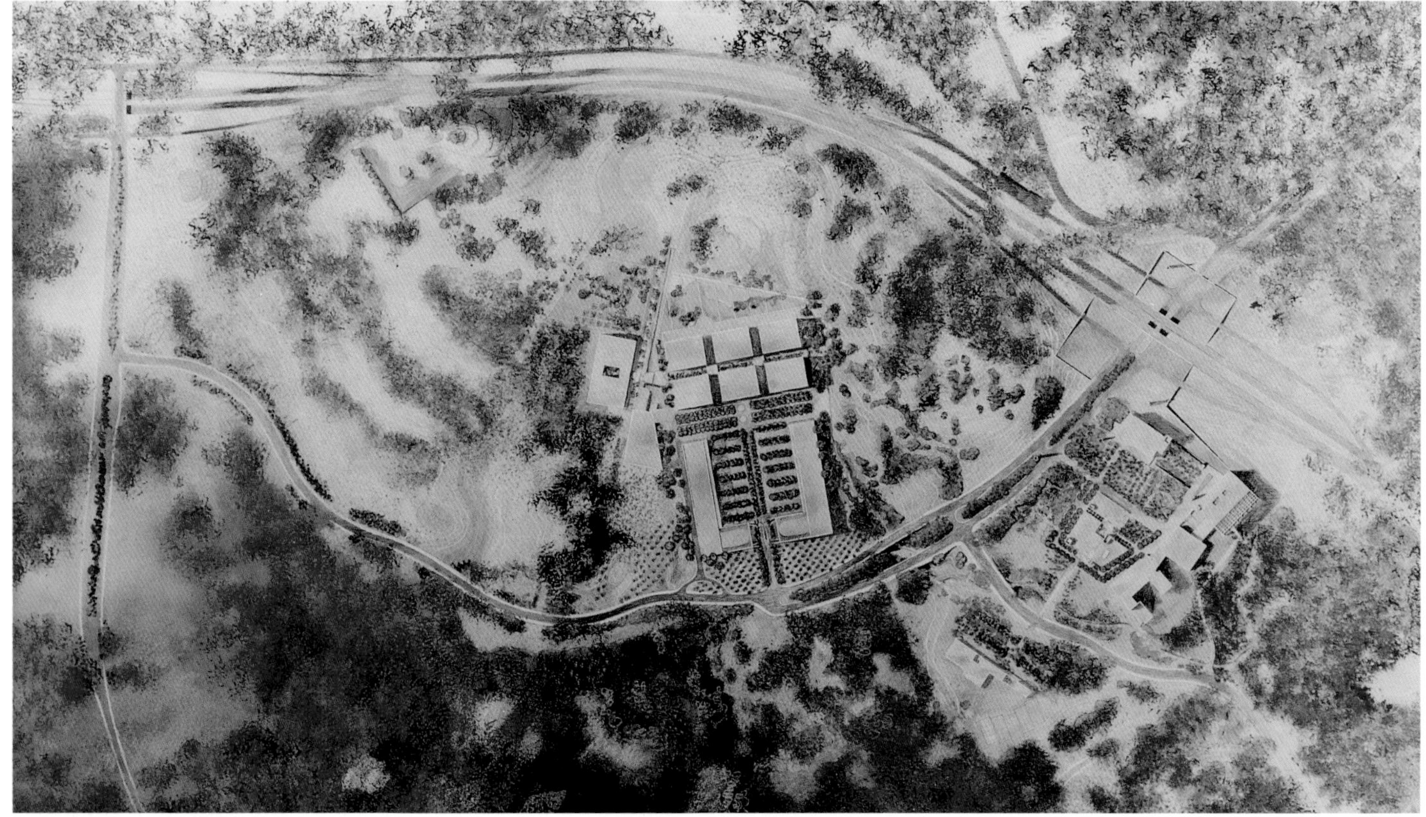
5

4 Parking garage
5 Rendered site plan
6 Detail of landscape feature
7 Detail of the facade

6

7

8 Ground-floor plan
9 Pedestrian precinct
10 "Impluvia" along central pedestrian street

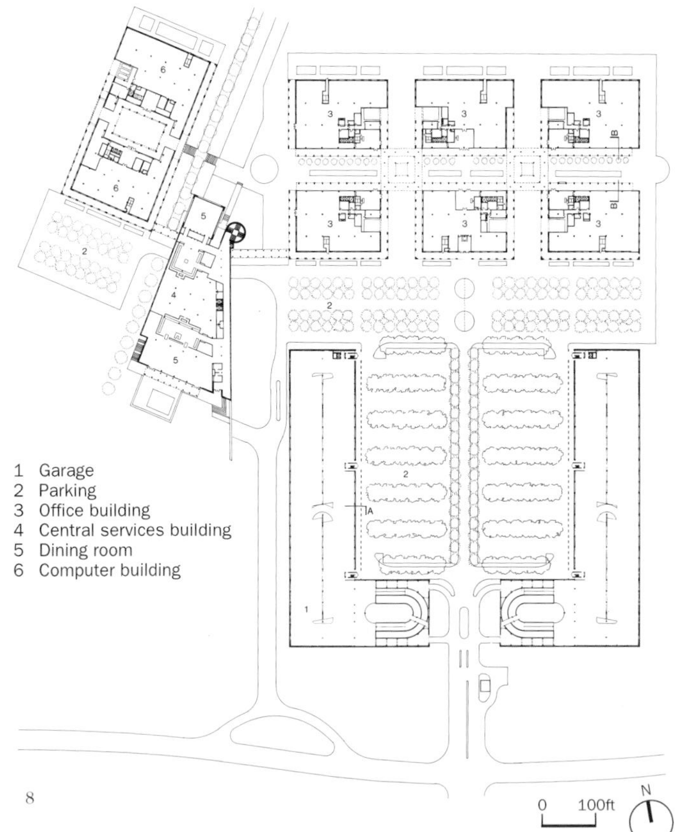

8

9

10

11 Precast concrete "porch"/arcade along pedestrian street
12 View to computer building
13 Office complex overlooking the prairie

11

12

13

14

15

14 Computer building
15 Dining pavilion
16 Detail of dining pavilion

16

17

18

17 South dining terrace with slatted awning
18 Interior of dining room
19 Main stair in dining pavilion

19

Columbus Center

Design/Completion 1989/1991
Coral Gables, Florida
Coral Gables Associates
Associate architects: The Nichols Partnership
279,000 square feet offices/retail
290,000 square feet parking
Plaster stucco exterior, clay tile roof, decorative tiles

Composed of offices, retail space, and parking, this center was designed in the context of the City Plan of Coral Gables, developed in the 1920s by the enlightened entrepreneur George Merrick. The plan set the stage for a Mediterranean-style community with a vibrant town center of unified design, lushly landscaped residential boulevards, and communal amenities.

To meet the rising demand for commercial space in the Gables, Columbus Center was built in accordance with a proscriptive zoning ordinance that follows Merrick's romantic vision. With its thirteen-story tower, the building establishes a new gateway into the city. The complex steps down toward the town center with an eight-story element, culminating in a park with a pool and gazebo at grade level. A planted trellis along the top of the screen wall conceals an 850-car parking structure and creates a transition to the offices above.

"By abstracting the Venetian characteristics of piazza, varied massing, stucco, barrel tile roofs, and the saturated hues of the Mediterranean, Columbus Center seeks a scale consistent with its surroundings and a sense of place." Paul Broches, FAIA

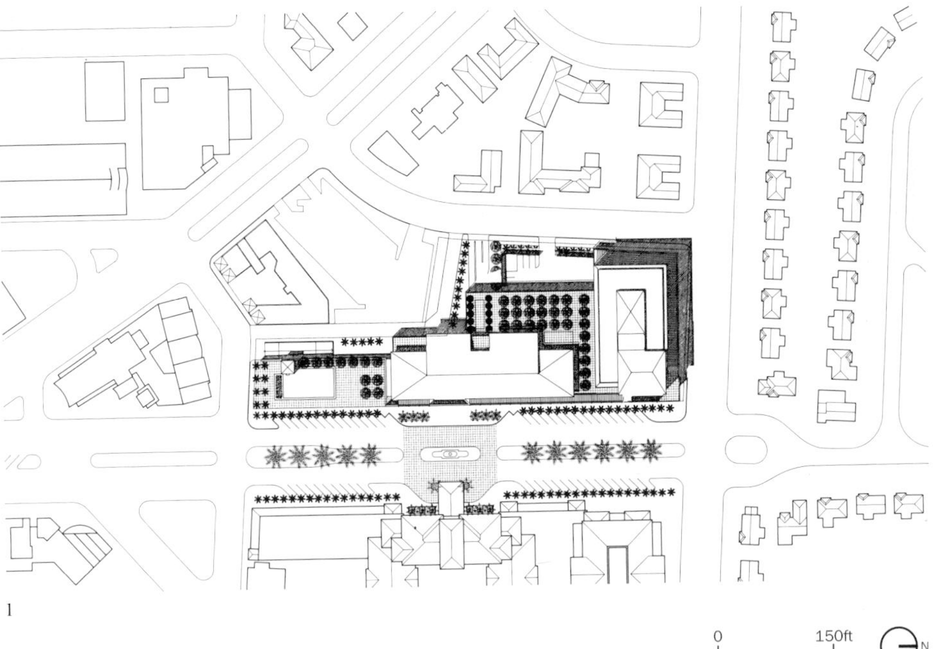

1

2

1 Site plan
2 View across reflecting pool
3 North tower

3

4 Aerial view of master plan
5 View from the south-east
6 View from the south

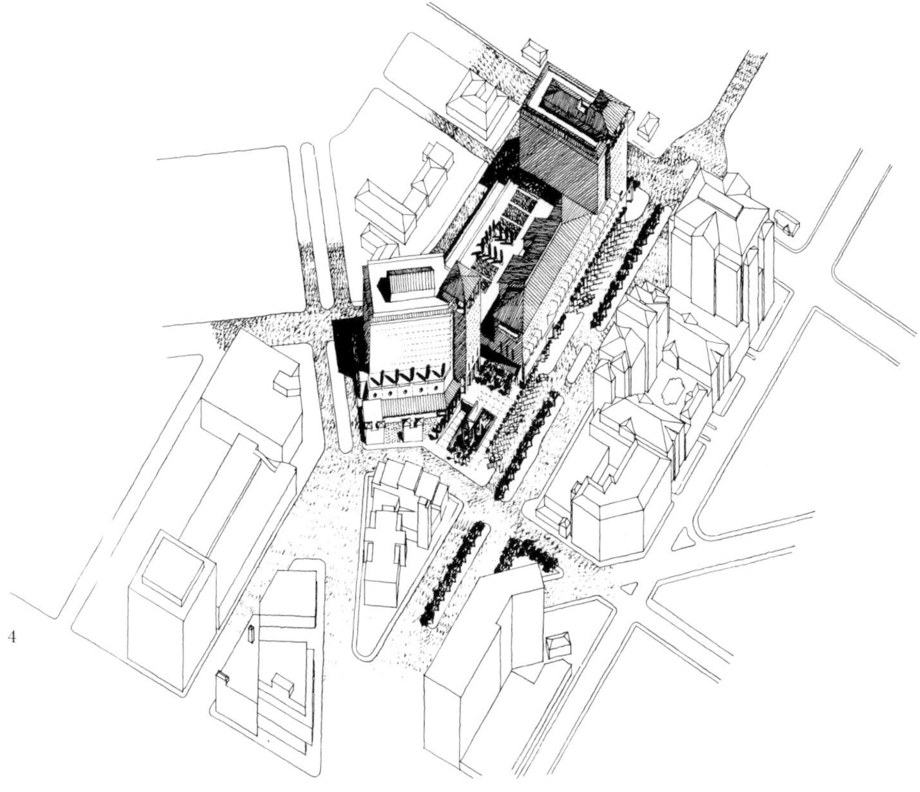

4

5

6

7 East elevation
8 South elevation
9 Tower main entry

7

8

9

10

10 Parking structure
11 South plaza
12 View to retail arcade
13 Detail at transition from parking structure base to office tower

11

12

13

14

14 Roof top garden
15 North tower lobby

15

The Lighthouse Inc. Headquarters

Design/Completion 1990/1994
New York, New York
The Lighthouse Inc.
170,000 square feet
Buff-colored brick with stone and glass accents
Maple, terrazzo, stainless steel interior finishes

The Lighthouse Inc. is the world's leading organization for vision impairment research and outreach. The new headquarters program includes a vision center, a child development center and pre-school, conference and education center with a 237-seat theater/auditorium, music school, library, technology center for job training, classrooms and offices, and an institute for applied research.

Public spaces are organized along the busy streetfront on 59th Street. To encourage wider public use and after-hours functions, the three-story Conference Center is located at the base of the building and interconnected by a prominent, central staircase. Offices and administration areas on the middle floors feature a clear plan organization with consistency from floor to floor to facilitate movement through the building, an especially important feature for people who are blind or partially sighted. The top floors contain the executive offices and the boardroom.

"The solution reflects the Lighthouse philosophy of 'mainstreaming' people with disabilities by being open, accessible, and an integral part of the urban fabric."
Steven M. Goldberg, FAIA

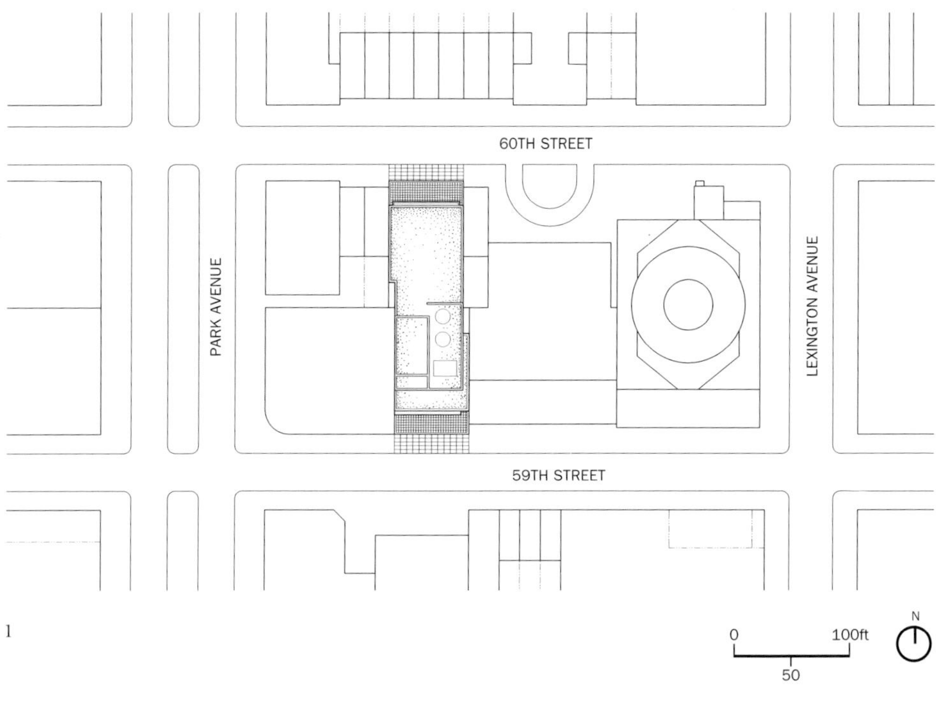

1

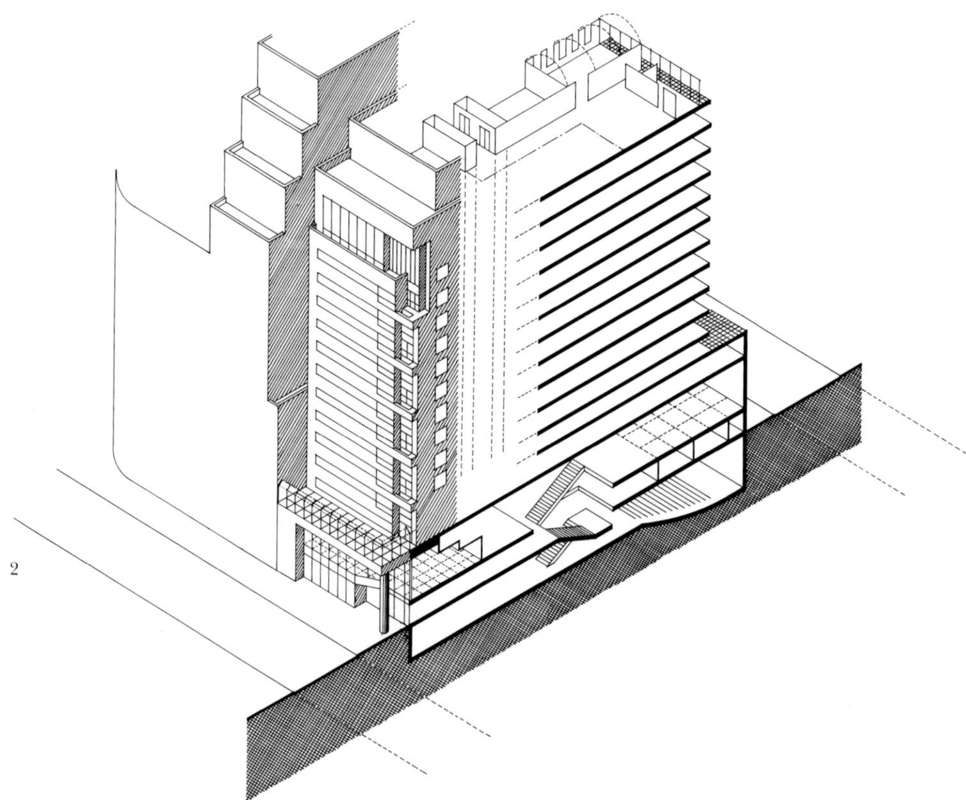

2

1 Site plan
2 Isometric projection
3 South-east corner

3

4

4 59th Street elevation looking west
5 Main entry with cafeteria above
6 60th street elevation looking south-east
7 Main entry with retail store

The Lighth

5

6

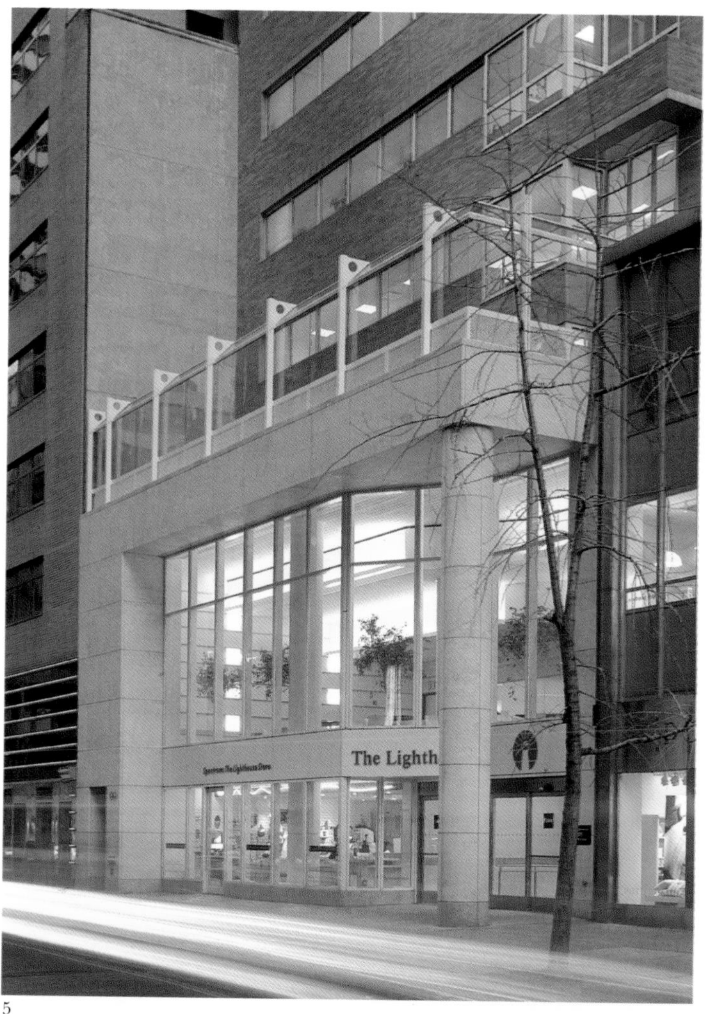

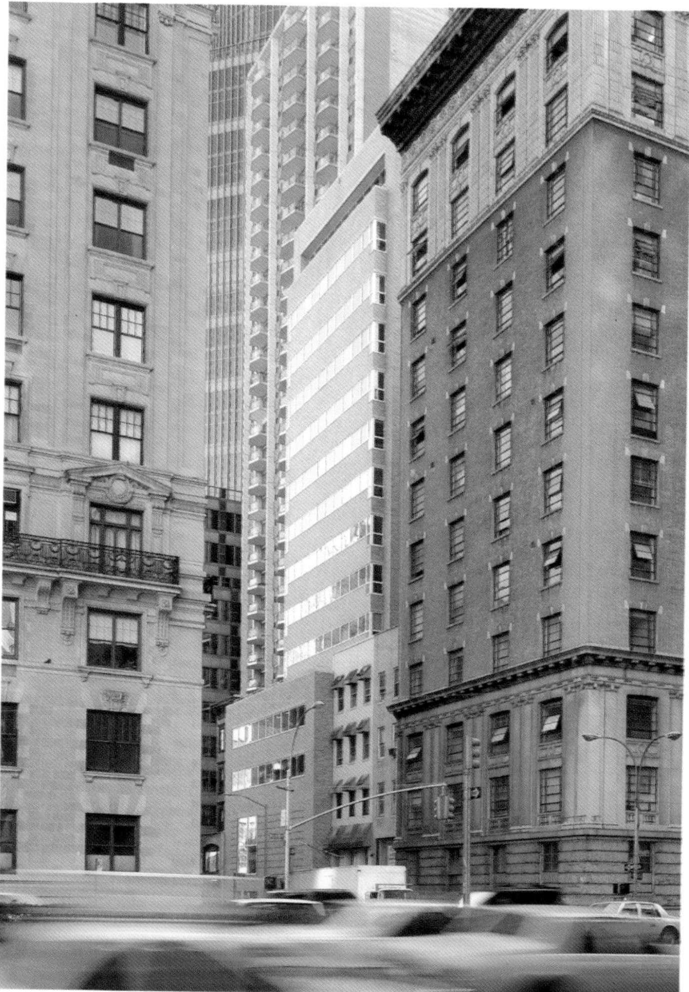

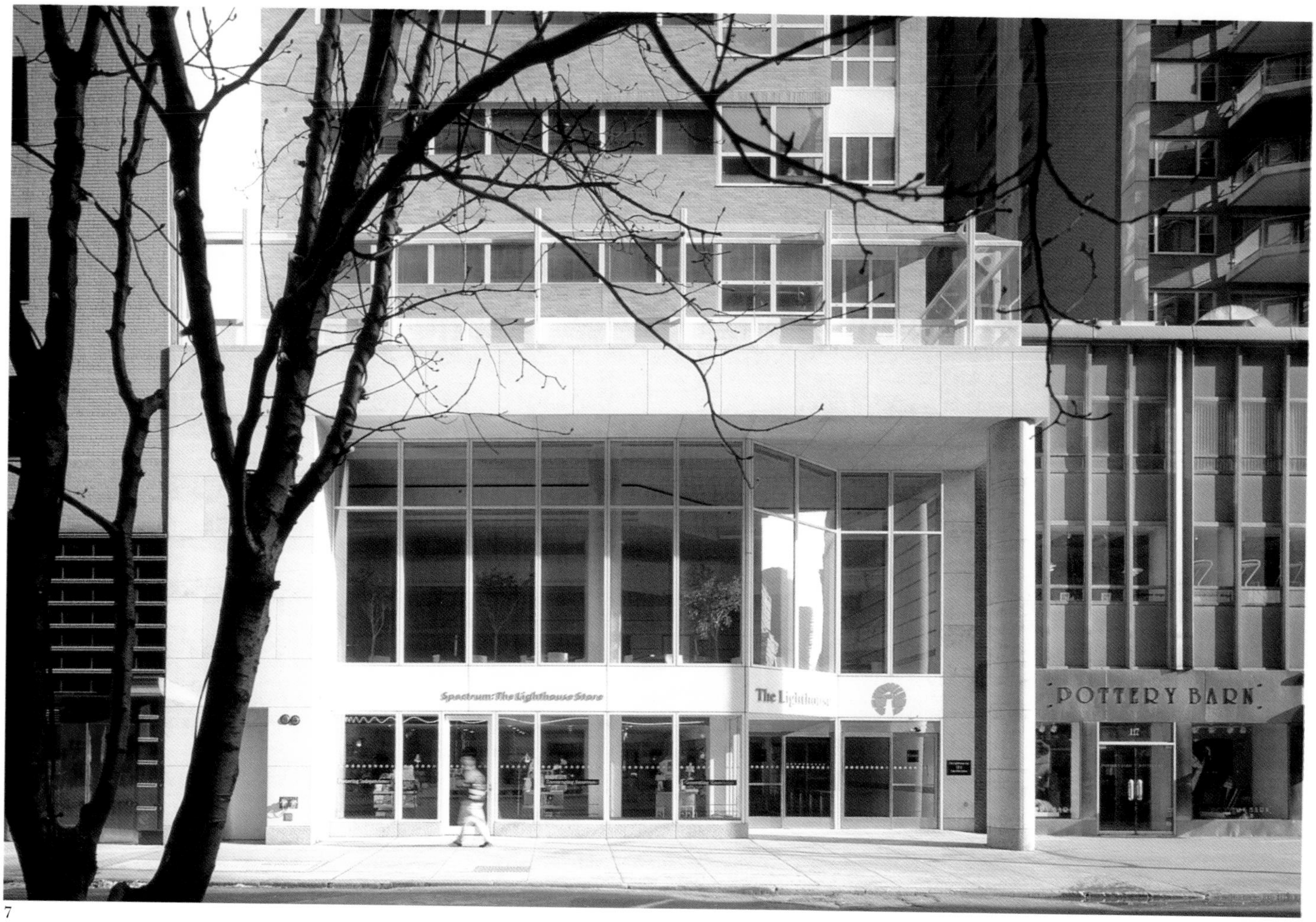
Spectrum: The Lighthouse Store
The Lighthouse
POTTERY BARN

7

8 Main entrance lobby
9 Entrance portico
10 Curved seating in the lobby
11 Tactile maps at main reception desk
12 Detail of steps
13 Detail of main reception desk
14 Stair to upper lobby

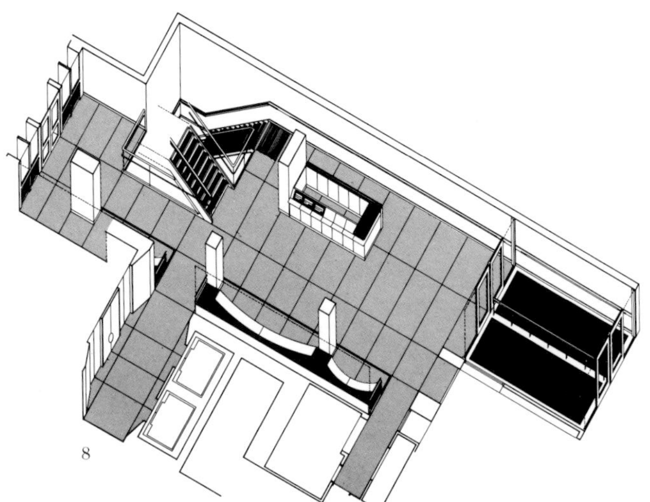

8

9

10

11

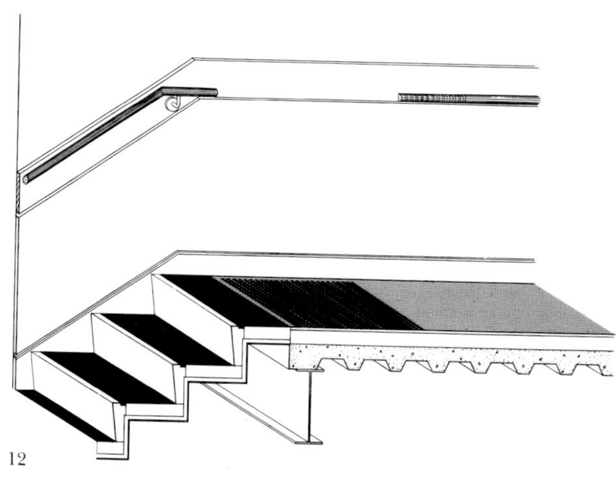

12

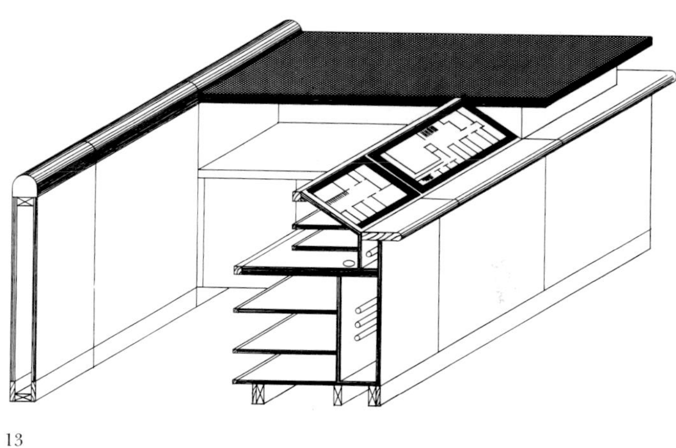

13

14

15

15 Main stair with Sol Lewitt "Styrofoam Installation"
16 View to lower auditorium lobby

16

17

18

17 237-seat auditorium
18 Cafeteria
19 Boardroom with cove ceiling
20 Multi-purpose room

19

20

21 Basement-floor plan
22 First-floor plan
23 Second-floor plan
24 Typical office floor reception
25 Child development center corridor
26 CDC bathroom
27 Enclosed outdoor play area
28 CDC training/play area

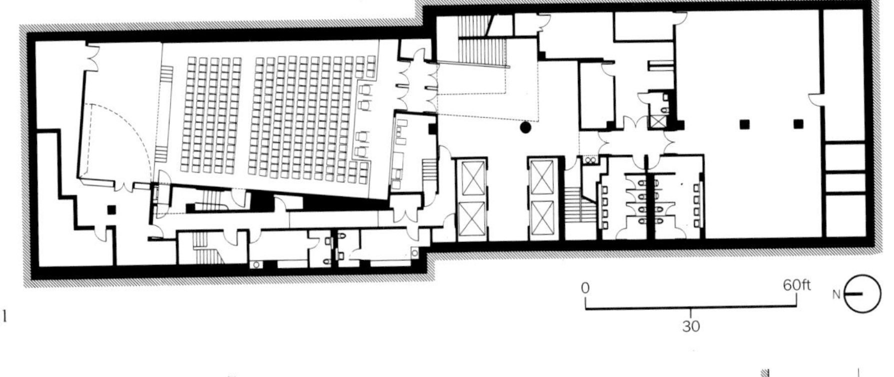

21

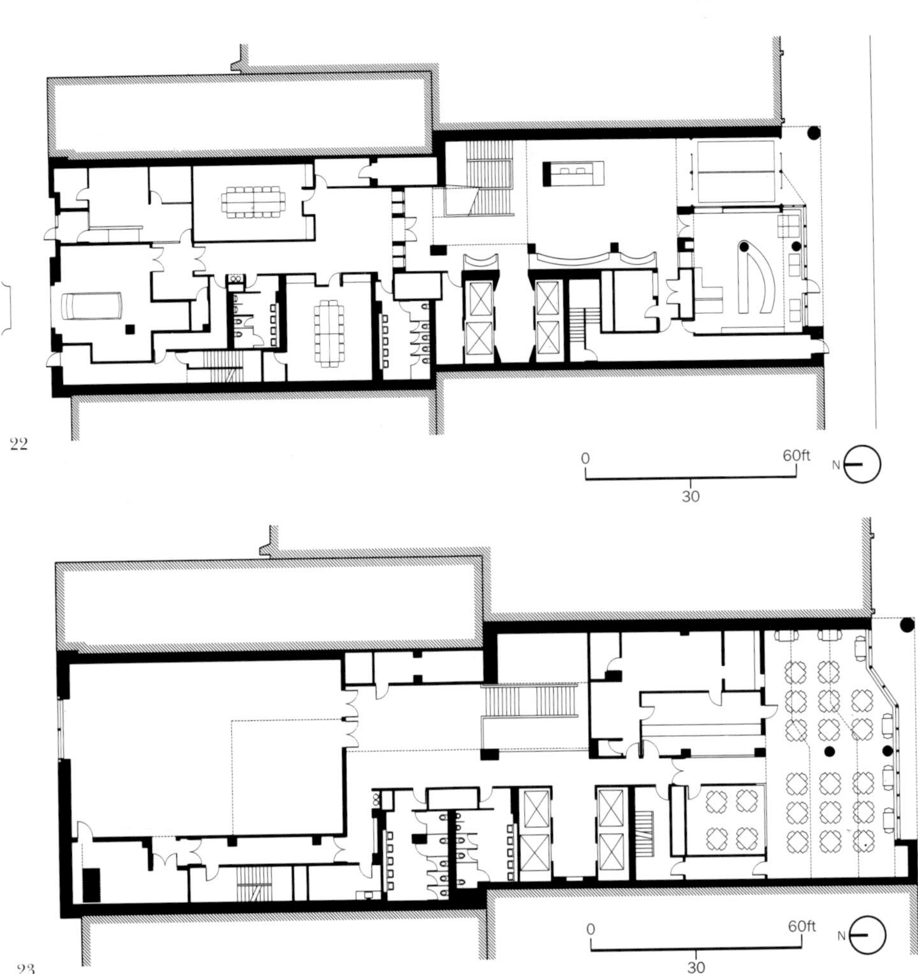

22

23

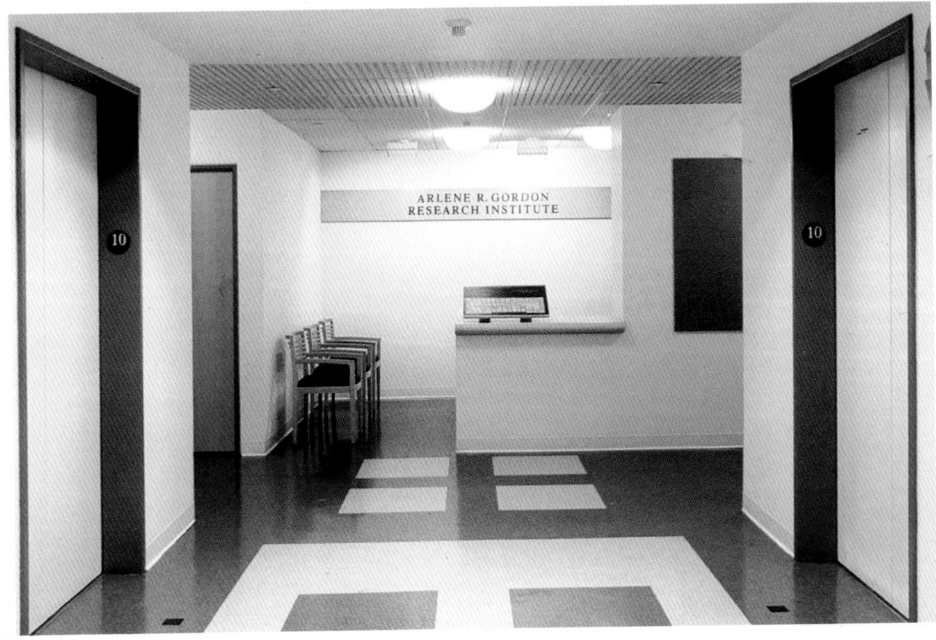

24

25

26

27

28

PUBLIC SPACES/PLACES

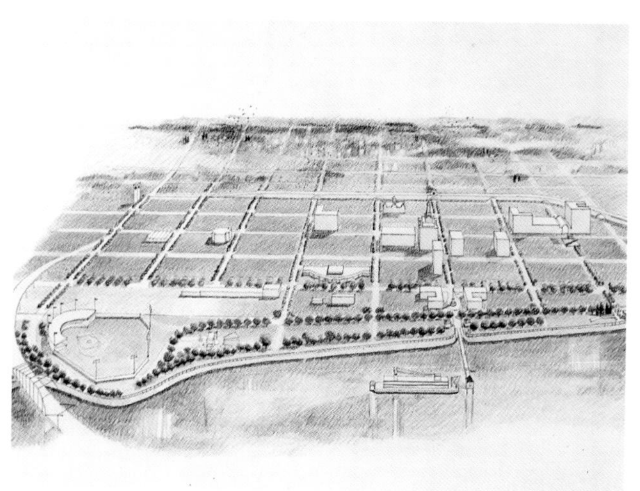

Hudson View East Residential Development

Design/Completion 1985/1987
New York, New York
Battery Park City Authority
116,000 square feet
Pink buff vetter stone, Cherokee granite, ornamental vetter stone frieze, blue glazed brick

This 110-unit, 18-story project is part of the housing sector of Battery Park City, a 92-acre mixed-use district in lower Manhattan. The site offers spectacular views of the Hudson River to the west and views of lower Manhattan to the east. Design guidelines, oriented toward capturing the spirit of more traditional New York residential neighborhoods, mandated adherence to streetwall requirements on two edges of the site, a two-story stone base, and a lively treatment of the top of the building.

The bulk of the apartments on the east side are configured in a series of vertical setbacks which provide corner windows and enhance the views and feeling of spaciousness. A cascading east facade is an animated counterpoint to the more uniform north and west facades.

"Within the context of the design guidelines, we introduced a Modernist palette: blue tile instead of limestone for expression lines, richly colored Kasota stone instead of limestone for the base, and expansive instead of smaller segmented windows for the apartments." Steven M. Goldberg, FAIA

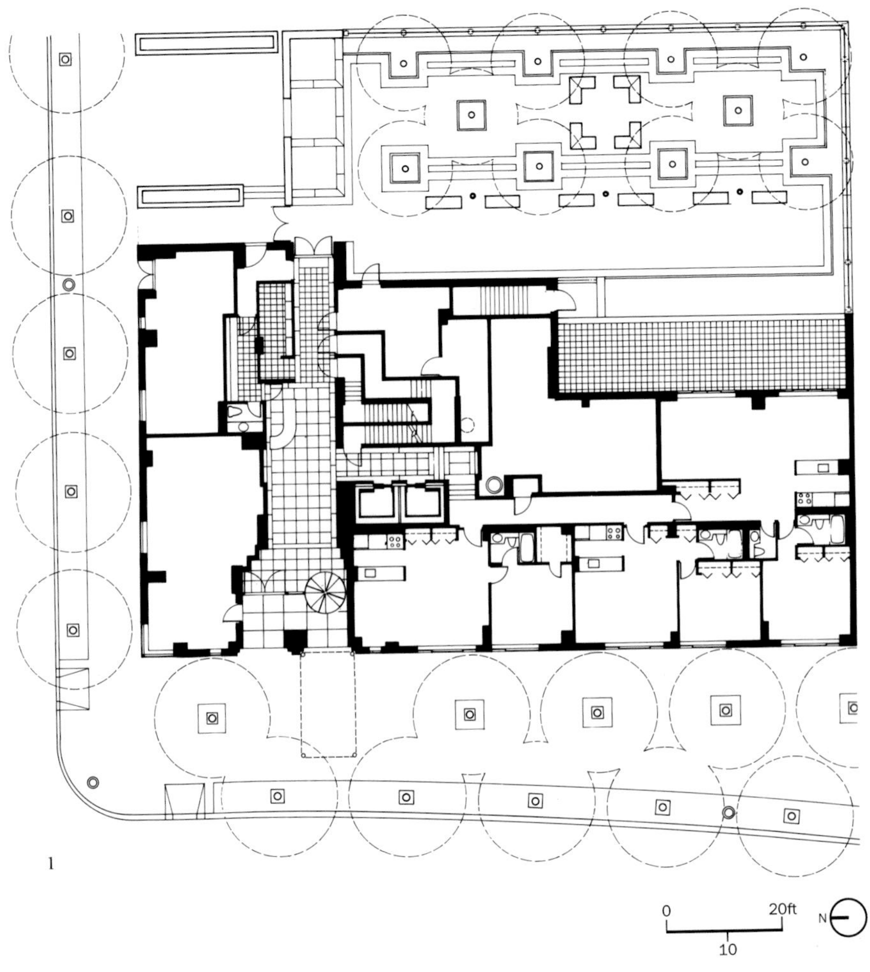

1

2

1 Ground-floor plan
2 Entrance view
3 View of west facade

3

4

5

6

4 West facade
5 Detail of base
6 Lobby
7 View looking north-east

7

Davenport Downtown Plan and River Center Plaza

Design/Completion 1985/1986
Davenport, Iowa
City of Davenport, and Visiting Artists Inc.
Associate: Elyn Zimmerman, Artist
Winning competition submission

This small midwestern city, located along the banks of the Mississippi River, is composed of landmarks, river history, open vistas, and intimate spaces which together present a range of tactile, aural, and visual experiences. The Downtown Plan aims to create a dynamic and urban riverfront which amplifies these vital qualities.

To provide the impetus for development of the central business district, the proposed River Center Plaza is elevated several feet above the surrounding sidewalks. Arcaded buildings are positioned on its east and west boundaries. The plaza is diagonally split from north-east to south-west by a metaphoric river—a symbol of the genesis of the city.

Terraced stone shelves mark periodic changes in the river's course. An allee of trees marches up the main axis and across the plaza, bridges the watercourse and terminates at the entrance to River Center, forming a visual link between the plaza and the Mississippi River.

"The metaphoric river traversing the plaza is an imagined geology, a tributary river, to remind Davenport of its now lost connection to the once vital Mississippi." Paul Broches, FAIA

1

2

1 Aerial view of the downtown
2 The metaphoric river
3 Allee to the river
4 View toward the Mississippi River
5 Plan of the plaza

3

"...AND THEN YOU HAVE THE SHINING RIVER, WINDING HERE AND THERE AND YONDER, ITS SWEEP INTERRUPTED AT INTERVALS BY CLUSTERS OF WOODED ISLANDS THREADED BY SILVER CHANNELS, AND YOU HAVE GLIMPSES OF DISTANT VILLAGES, ASLEEP UPON CAPES; AND OF STEALTHY RAFTS SLIPPING ALONG IN THE SHADE OF THE FOREST WALLS; AND OF WHITE STEAMERS VANISHING AROUND REMOTE POINTS. AND IT IS ALL AS TRANQUIL AND REPOSEFUL AS DREAMLAND, AND HAS NOTHING THIS-WORLDLY ABOUT IT – NOTHING TO HANG A FRET OR A WORRY UPON."

– Mark Twain

4

5

Intertech Corporation, Office Development Master Plan

Design/Completion 1989/1990
Louden, Virginia
Intertech Corporation

This 275-acre parcel is adjacent to the Leesburg Pike near Washington, DC in an area of gently rolling hills, open farmland and wooded stream valleys. The master plan establishes parameters for building locations and sizes, circulation, parking, service, recreational facilities, open spaces, landscaping, and areas to be preserved in their natural condition.

The selected concept uses visual forms from the native agricultural tradition to organize and lend identity to the site. A large square meadow in the center provides a focus for a surrounding grid of building and parking parcels. The remainder of the potential development site area is overlaid with native hedgerows organizing both future development parcels and open space required by zoning.

The hedgerows provide shade and visual order to the development. Between hedgerows, the open areas receive a variety of agricultural plantings yielding seasonal changes in color and texture.

"As the region changes from farms to corporate office parks, this development will preserve the 200-year-old historic and cultural memory of the land."
Jan Keane, FAIA

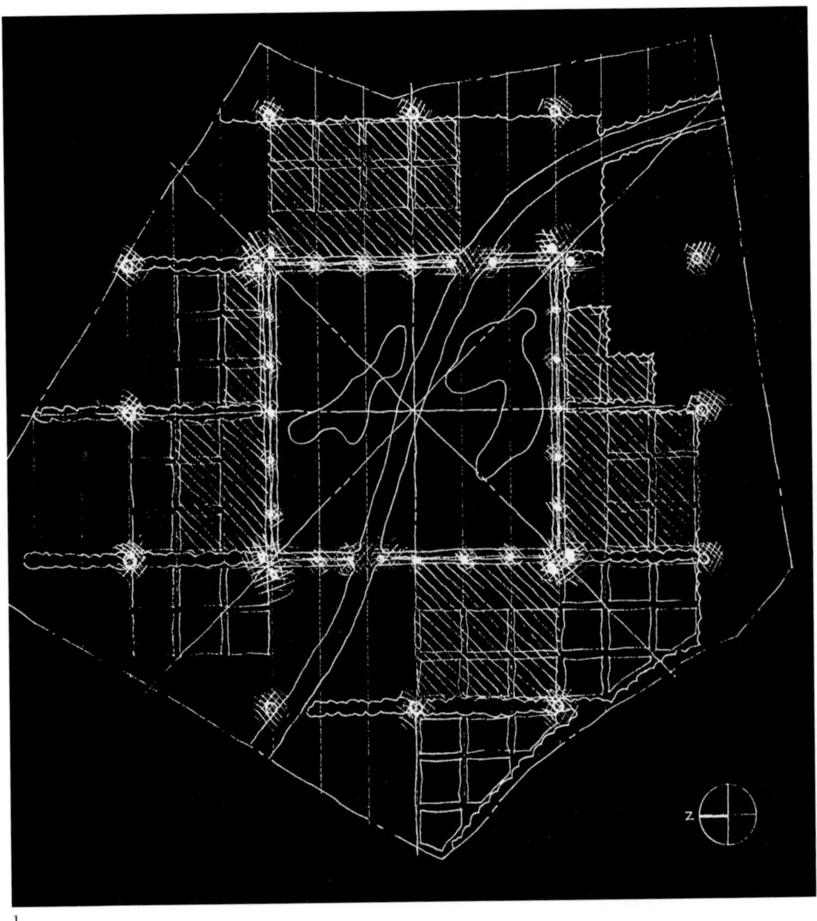

1

2

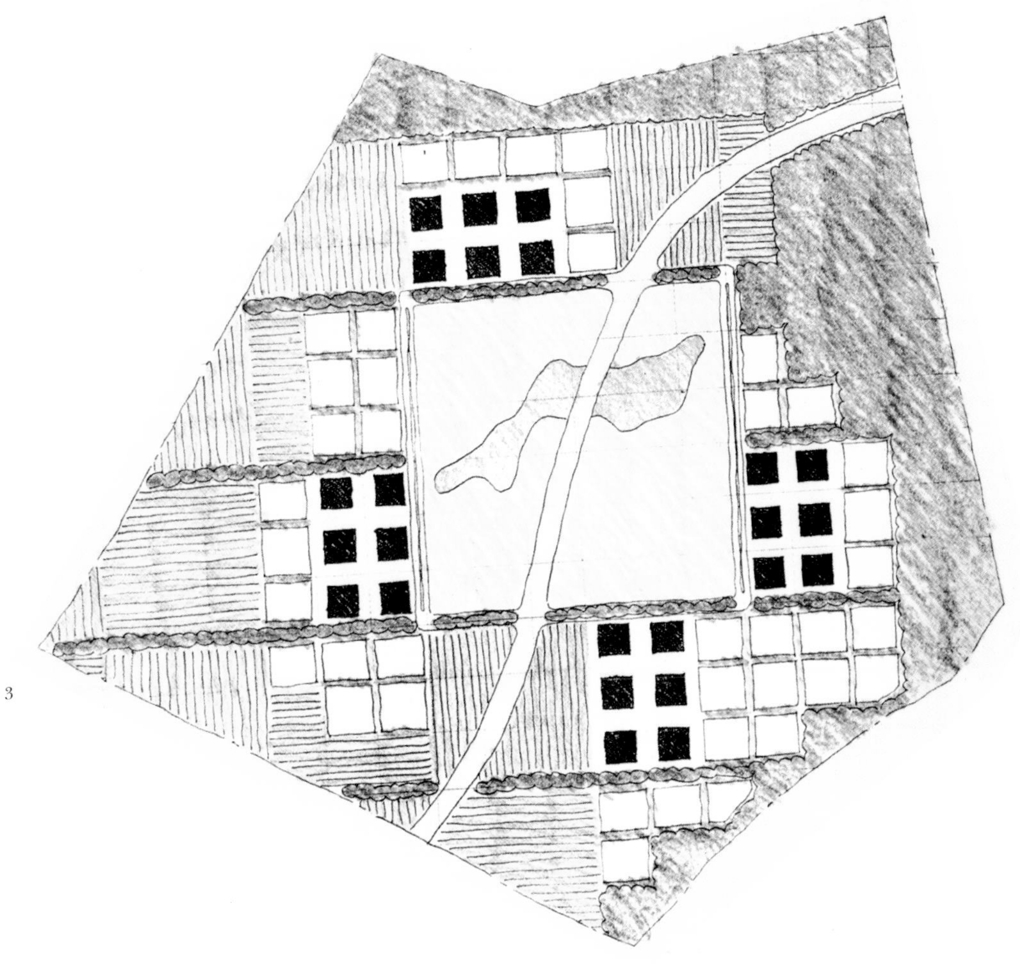

3

4

1 Lighting master plan
2 Context plan
3 Development master plan
4 Aerial perspective

St Joseph's College Comprehensive Plan

Design/Completion 1993/1994
Patchogue, New York
St Joseph's College

Since the acquisition of a 23-acre site in 1978, this campus has grown considerably from its enrollment of 350 students. This strong growth has put pressure on all aspects of the physical campus: buildings, playing fields and parking. This 10-year comprehensive plan seeks to define locations for urgently needed new buildings and create a hierarchy of spaces to give the campus a clear organizing structure.

A quadrangle formed by an original high school building and a recently completed library is at the heart of a new campus identity. The siting of several buildings in the future will reinforce the boundaries of the quadrangle. The most imminent of these new buildings is a new physical activities facility, a focal point for the creation of the plan. Existing pedestrian circulation will be strengthened to link all campus buildings and the parking area in a clear and simple fashion.

"This plan sets the limits for growth and the desirable architectural language of future buildings to appropriately reflect the values of the institution."
Paul Broches, FAIA

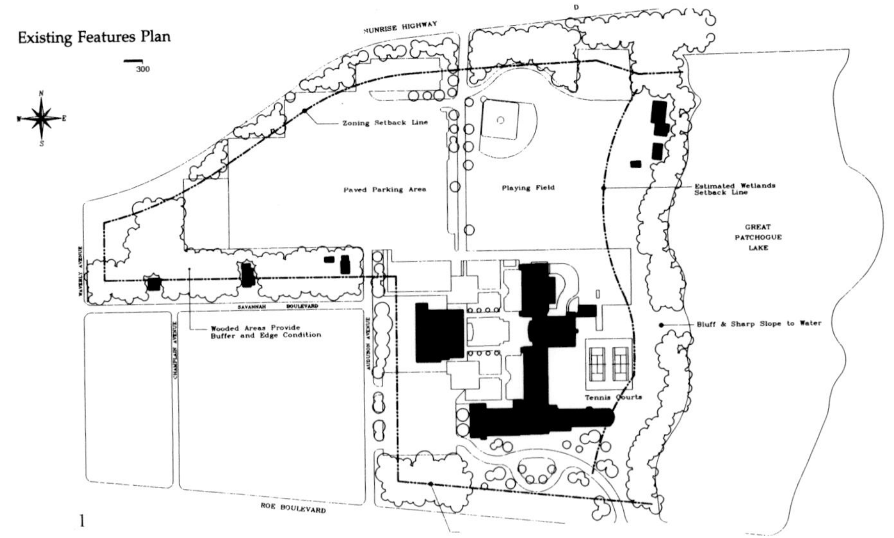

1

2

3

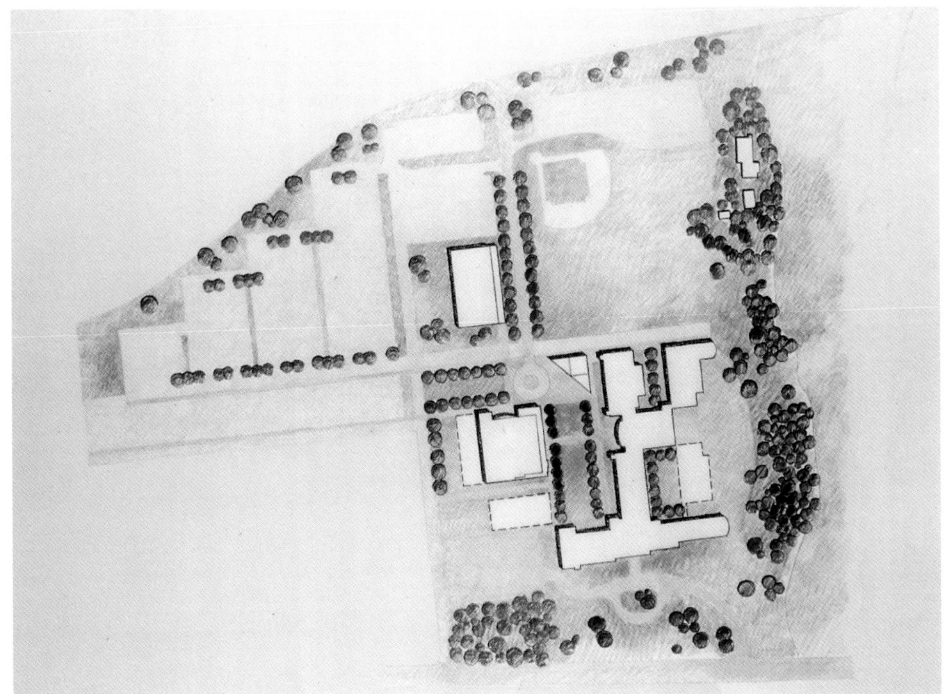

4

1 Site plan
2 View toward student center
3 View of sports/recreation center
4 Illustrated site plan

Southampton College Master Plan, Long Island University

Design/Completion 1993/1994
Southampton, New York
Southampton College, Long Island University

Long Island University's Southampton College encompasses a number of small buildings randomly placed on a 100-acre rolling tract of land. A master plan was undertaken to establish an organizing framework and a clear identity for the campus which had developed haphazardly over the years.

A new circulation system defines and amplifies residential and academic precincts: an elliptical roadway unifies disparate dormitory buildings while a north–south curving entry road and two east–west roads provide the framework for an academic community. The area between the two precincts, which contains the student center and administration building, becomes the "village green," the heart of the campus. Proposed new buildings and additions to existing buildings reinforce the new organization.

"The relatively simple superimposition of a road network creates a front door to the campus as well as a front door to its major buildings." Paul Broches, FAIA

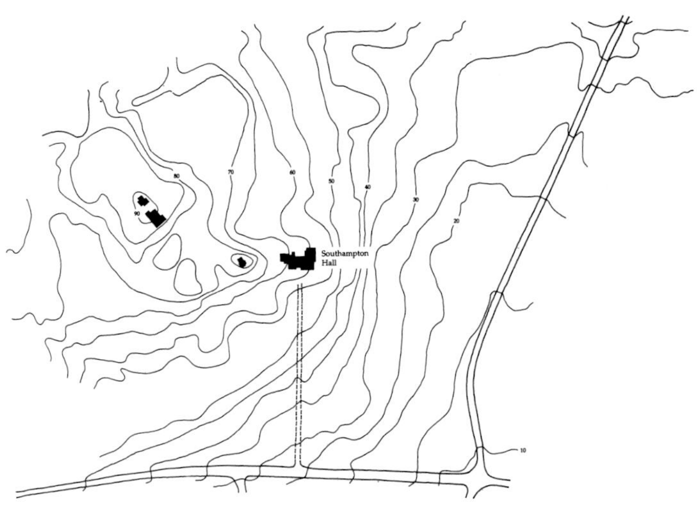

1

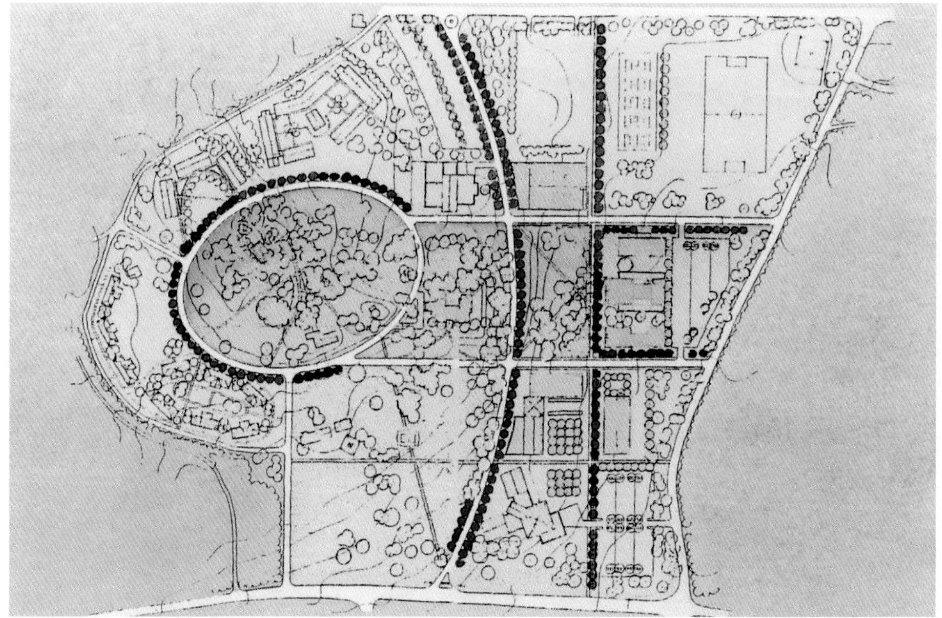

2

1 Southampton Hall
2 New master plan
3 Existing road network and buildings, 1994
4 Proposed site improvements
5 Aerial view of master plan

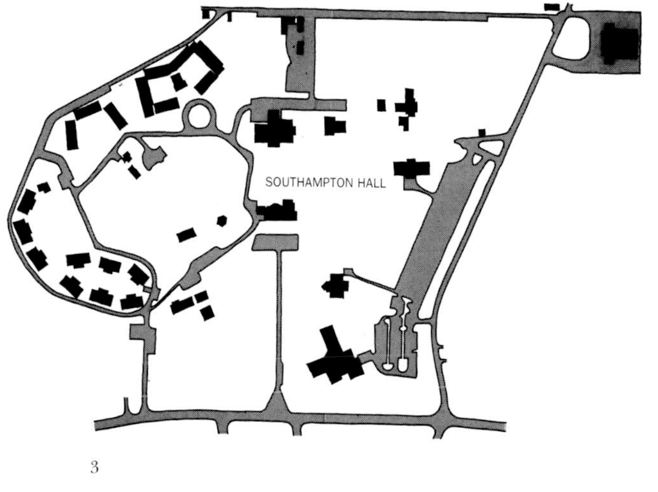

3

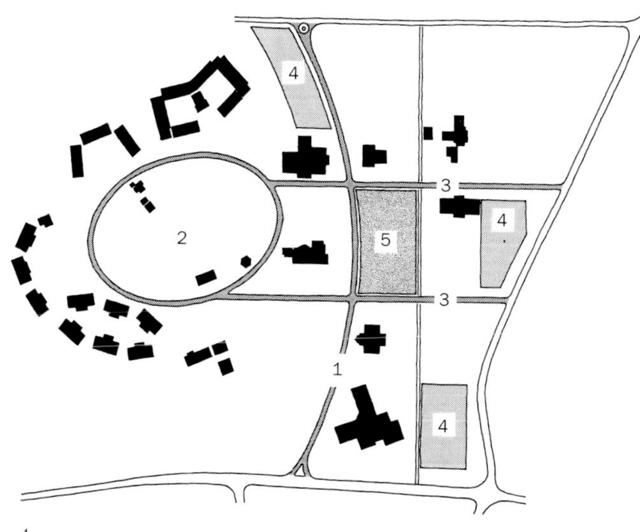

4

1 Create north–south through road
2 Create ellipse to organize dormitory zone
3 Create east–west links
4 Reorganize parking
5 Create central quadrangle
to organize academic buildings

5

The Belvedere, Battery Park City

Design/Completion 1991/1995
New York, New York
Battery Park City Authority
Associate firm: Child Associates Inc. Landscape Architects
1.6 acres
Dakota granite, English oak trees, honey locust trees, teak and stainless steel railings

As the last centrally located undeveloped open space in Battery Park City, this site is a keystone: it both connects and supports the entire composition of waterfront at the edge of the Hudson River in lower Manhattan.

Primary elements of the park include: an elevated platform area with a densely planted bosque of English oak trees; a belvedere with honey locust trees; an esplanade; and battered stone wall, steps, and ramps which separate the two levels.

The battered, serpentine wall and railing provide a continuous seating surface throughout the park. Broad steps and ramps are cut into the wall to connect the two levels. At the bosque, steps 80 feet wide provide areas for sitting and sunning. Two striking multi-story stainless steel light pylons, designed by the noted sculptor Martin Puryear, serve as distinctive markers of the park as well as provide a symbolic welcome to those arriving by ferry.

"We wanted to create a civic 'place' that was both formal and informal and that provided a seamless connection between the Olmstedian Hudson River Park to the north and the plaza of the World Financial Center to the east."
Steven M. Goldberg, FAIA

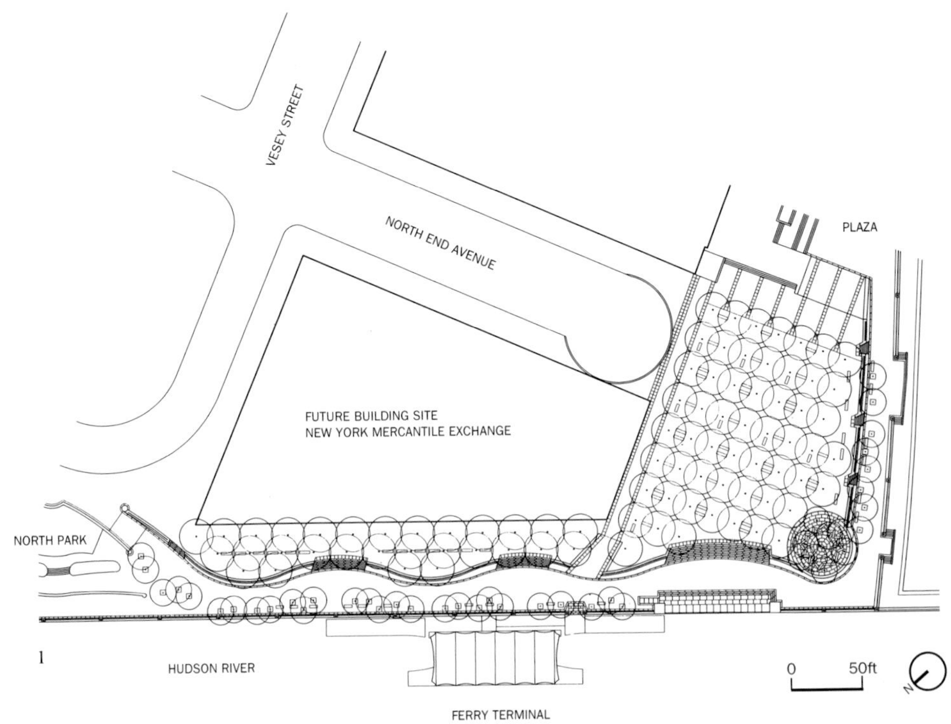

1

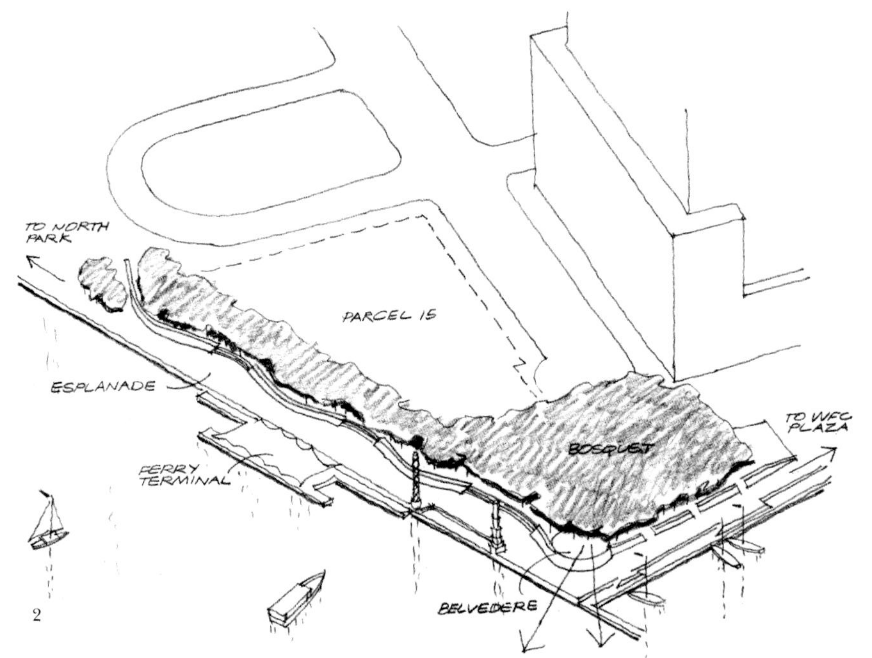

2

1 Site plan
2 Site axonometric sketch
3 View toward Statue of Liberty

3

4

5

4 View looking west
5 Arrival from Trans-Hudson ferry to World Financial Center
6 Esplanade looking west
7 Esplanade looking east

6

7

8 Axonometric of the site
9 Grand stair, river viewing area
10 View along the esplanade
11 Reclining on the wall
12 Stone detail at grand stair

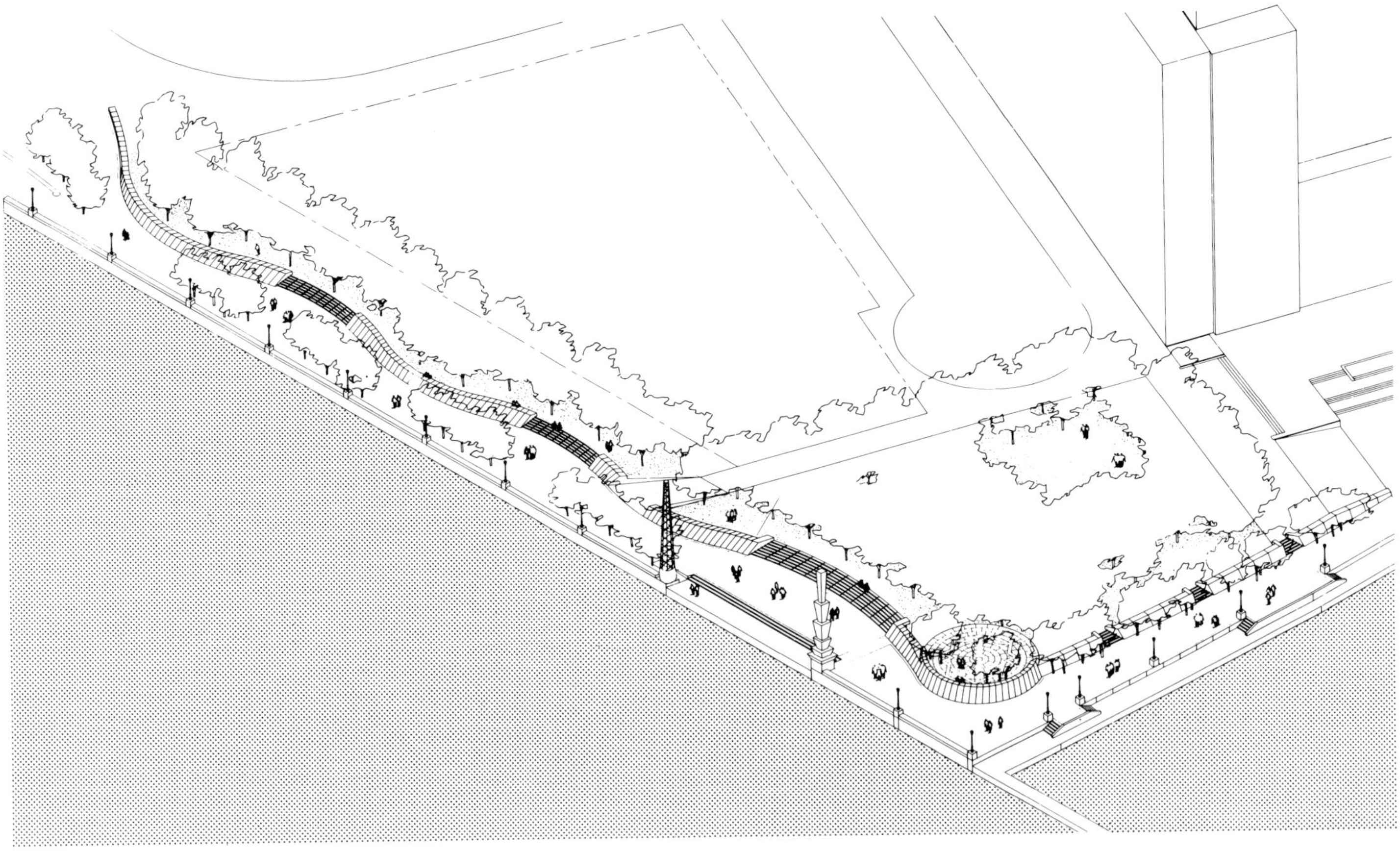

8

9

10

11

12

13

14

13 View from the west
14 View from the belvedere to the Statue of Liberty
15 Stainless steel pylons by Martin Puryear
16 View south to Statue of Liberty
17 Pylons at dusk looking south on the river
18 Detail of open-weave pylon

15

16

17

18

FIRM PROFILE

Biographies

MITCHELL/GIURGOLA ARCHITECTS

The master plans, buildings and projects presented in this volume were executed over the ten-year period from 1986 to 1996. The work reflects Mitchell/Giurgola's continuing tradition of creating buildings of accommodation, spatial generosity, a strong sense of order, and a spirit of serenity. Most of the 31 projects presented have been carried out by the five partners during a period of transition during which they succeeded Romaldo Giurgola and Ehrman B. Mitchell to lead the firm.

Since Professor Giurgola's move to Australia, the office has continued to serve public, institutional, academic, and corporate clients, consistently maintaining a program-derived and site-sensitive approach to design. The success of the firm is measured both by its buildings and by the level of service offered to its clients, more than two-thirds of whom have long-standing relationships with the firm and have commissioned multiple projects.

Partners Paul Broches, Steven Goldberg, Jan Keane, John Kurtz and Mark Markiewicz bring diverse perspectives to their work. Through frequent on-the-boards deliberations and peer review, a shared vision emerges in each project. All five partners have successfully incorporated and built upon the founders' design philosophy and working style in their own work. The designs created by the group are richer for the collaborative process they have embraced.

The studio setting at Mitchell/Giurgola was an excellent training ground for the current partners and has provided a similar foundation for its associates and staff. A tightly knit working method and design philosophy has been maintained by limiting the size of the office and by assuring substantial and consistent participation in all projects by the principals.

The motivating force for setting a design direction draws upon the characteristics that make each client unique. The diversity of design solutions reflects this approach. The common threads in the work derive from the highly complex programs given to the architects. The synthesis of numerous potentially conflicting demands is a familiar process for the partners as they view building elements as fragments of a larger whole, woven together in much the same way as the fabric of the city. The Mitchell/Giurgola portfolio is replete with projects which are complex in their programs and site conditions, varied in their materials and appearance, yet simple, dignified and clear in their execution.

The partners do not favor the imposition of any particular style on their work. The form of a given project evolves in direct response to the program and its specific site characteristics. Ultimately, each building emerges from its context to take on a presence and definition that is unique. It is the tension between these seemingly contradictory qualities that defines the Mitchell/Giurgola signature. The firm's designs are a result of a personal architectural expression informed by history, culture, and human behavior.

In summary, it may be said that architecture for Mitchell/Giurgola is fundamentally about the translation of social enterprise into an expressive and dignified built form. The measure of its success is, in the first instance, the way in which it is appropriated by its inhabitants; and secondly, the degree to which it is imbued with a specific identity and a timeless and memorable presence.

PAUL BROCHES
FAIA

Paul Broches joined Mitchell/Giurgola Architects in 1971 after earning his Master of Architecture degree from Columbia University in 1970 and Bachelor of Arts degree in 1967. He was named an associate in 1976, made Manager of the New York office in 1977, and became a partner in 1980.

Mr Broches has led the master planning efforts for numerous institutional clients and has collaborated on the design of both new and adaptive re-use projects. In addition, he is active in design management and personnel issues. He has a particular interest in, and has frequently spoken on, the collaborative process, particularly on the subject of public art. He worked on the winning submission in a national competition for a collaborative project with the artist Elyn Zimmerman. Other projects have involved the sculptor Richard Fleischner and the painter Valerie Jaudon. He served as an advisor to the National Endowment for the Arts' Public Art Policy Project; as a symposium panelist on "Art in Public Places" at the University of Massachusetts; and as a member of the Urban Design Task Force Advisory Committee of the American Planning Association.

Mr Broches was elected to the College of Fellows of the American Institute of Architects in 1991 and has served the AIA at both the national and local level in many capacities, including membership on a joint AIA/New York City School Construction Authority Task Force to raise the design standards of the construction of public schools. He has also chaired the awards program and serves on the New York Board of Architects/Designers/Planners for Social Responsibility (ADSPR/NY). Mr Broches has served on design award juries for New York State, Arkansas, and the International Association of Lighting Design.

Mr Broches has been a visiting critic and juror at Columbia University (1973–present), New Jersey College of Architecture (1981–present), Tulane University (1976), and Virginia Polytechnic Institute (1974). He is registered in ten US states, as well as in the Australian Capital Territory, and holds a certificate from the National Council of Architectural Registration Boards.

Mr Broches is the author of "La Arquitectura de Comunidad Agradable" in *TRAMA, Review of Architecture* (Ecuador), 1995; "Perspectives on Collaboration: The River Center Project" for the *Public Art Dialogue—Southeast*; "Going Public: A Field Guide to Development of Art in Public Places," a National Endowment for the Arts publication; "Implanter Un Nouveau Mode de Fabrication Automobile en Amerique du Nord" in *Conception des Espaces Industriels et Amelioration des Conditions de Travail* published by the University of Montreal; "Learning in Luxury, The New IBM Advanced Business Institute," in *Interspace 91* (with Mark Markiewicz); and a feature article on Mitchell/Giurgola in *The Encyclopedia of Architecture* published by John Wiley and Sons.

STEVEN M. GOLDBERG
FAIA

Steven M. Goldberg has taken an active role in design and urban planning issues throughout the USA and abroad. A frequent lecturer, Mr Goldberg was the 1995 Chair of the AIA National Committee on Design where he was responsible for guiding the activities of the committee, including their convention programs and national and international design conferences. His theme for 1995, "Urban Transformations," focused on Dallas/Fort Worth, Barcelona and Pittsburgh. In this capacity, he recently hosted a week-long symposium in Barcelona, Spain as well as moderating panels on "Understanding the GSA's Design Excellence Program" and the Architectural Firm Award at the AIA National Convention in Atlanta. In 1995, he was a keynote speaker at the Colegios de Arquitectos del Ecuador Global Day of the Architect in Quito, Ecuador; keynote speaker and juror for the 7th National Meeting for Students of Architecture in Queretaro, Mexico; and keynote speaker for the XIX Congress for La Federacion de Colegios de Arquitectos in Aguascalientes, Mexico.

After joining Mitchell/Giurgola in 1967, Mr Goldberg was named an associate in 1974 and a partner in 1980. In addition to his role as a collaborating designer on planning and building projects for institutional and commercial clients, he is actively involved in the management of the firm and the development of the practice. Mr Goldberg has been a visiting critic and juror at Parsons School of Design (1978, 1979), Rensselaer Polytechnic Institute (1994) and the University of North Carolina (1980), and a faculty member of the School of Architecture at Columbia University (1967–70). He earned a Master of Science degree in Urban Design from Columbia University in 1967 and Master of Architecture (1965) and Bachelor of Arts (1962) degrees from the University of Pennsylvania, where he was elected to Phi Beta Kappa.

Mr Goldberg was elected to the College of Fellows of the American Institute of Architects in 1991 and has served the AIA nationally in many capacities, including juror (R.S. Reynolds Memorial Award, 1991); Moderator (1995 Convention, "Understanding GSA's Design Excellence Program" and 1995 Architecture Firm Award); 1995 Chair and member of the National Committee on Design's Steering Committee (since 1989); and Chairman of the Awards Nominations Committee (1989–94). A well-respected design juror, Mr Goldberg has participated in design awards programs for, among others, the Houston Chapter/AIA (1996), the Pennsylvania Society of Architects (1995), the Wisconsin Society of Architects (1992), and the Philadelphia Chapter/AIA (1990).

He is the co-author of "The Lighthouse Headquarters: A National Model of Accessibility for People With Impaired Vision" with Jan Keane, and "Northern Light in a Museum" with Robert Shalkop (featured in *Museum News*), and author of "Light and Architecture Enhance Communication With Art," a feature in *Lighting Design and Application* magazine. He is also highly regarded for his collaborative efforts with artists, the most recent example being his work with Martin Puryear on the award-winning park, The Belvedere, in Battery Park City, and Sol Lewitt on the Lighthouse Headquarters in Manhattan.

JAN KEANE
FAIA

Since joining Mitchell/Giurgola in 1971, Jan Keane has contributed actively to the built work of the firm, particularly in the master planning and design of research laboratories, administrative offices and computer facilities. She was named an associate of the firm in 1978, a partner in 1980, and Administrative Partner in 1987. Ms Keane earned her Master of Architecture degree from Columbia University in 1971 and Bachelor of Arts degree from Vassar College in 1967.

Ms Keane has taken a leadership role in the firm not only as a design collaborator, but also as a day-to-day manager of operations. She was elected to the College of Fellows of the American Institute of Architects in 1995, having served as Treasurer of the New York Chapter from 1992 to 1994 and as a member of the Committee on the Environment, and the Finance Committee. She is currently Vice President of the New York Chapter of the AIA.

Her contributions to the profession include participation on design juries throughout the country, including the design awards programs for the Pennsylvania Society of Architects (1995), the Boston Society of Architects (1995), the Dallas Chapter/AIA (1989), the New England Regional Chapter/AIA (1988), and the International Association of Lighting Design (1984). She has also been a lecturer/juror at Columbia University (1976–81), Ball State University (1990), and Rensselaer Polytechnic Institute (1994). Ms Keane holds a Certificate from the National Council of Architectural Registration Boards and is registered in nine US states.

As a nationally recognized expert in the design of laboratories, Ms Keane has lectured widely on the planning and design of complex programmed buildings. She was a featured presenter on the Ciba Pharmaceuticals Division Life Sciences Building (the 1995 Lab of the Year) at the Pittsburgh Conference in New Orleans and the R&D Facilities: Innovative Designs, Cost-Effective Strategies Conference in San Diego; and on the RPI George M. Low Center for Industrial Innovation at the University Science & Research Facilities Conference in San Francisco. Ms Keane was the keynote speaker on "Adding Vision to Universal Design" at The Lighthouse Inc. and a featured lecturer at NeoCon 94 with a paper she co-authored entitled, "The Lighthouse Headquarters: A National Model of Accessibility for People With Impaired Vision."

JOHN M. KURTZ

AIA

John Kurtz joined Mitchell/Giurgola Architects in 1968, after earning his Bachelor of Arts and Master of Architecture degrees from the University of Pennsylvania in 1965 and 1967 respectively. He was named an associate of the firm in 1976 and a partner in 1987.

Mr Kurtz provides design leadership to project teams to extend their explorations and to maintain state-of-the-art technical standards. His input also assures consistency in the design of projects from conceptual design through detailed execution.

He has been involved with a wide range of commissions during his tenure, including a five-year residency in Canberra, Australia during the design and construction of the new Parliament House project. While in Australia, Mr Kurtz was active in the Royal Australian Institute of Architects/Canberra Chapter and since his return to New York has been active in the New York City Chapter of the American Institute of Architects.

Mr Kurtz's drawings are held in the permanent collections of the Centre Georges Pompidou in Paris and The Lighthouse Inc. in New York City. His design of a large tile mural was also installed at the University of Vermont, Stafford Hall in Burlington, Vermont.

In addition to registration in several US states, Mr Kurtz holds a certificate from the National Council of Architectural Registration Boards. Mr Kurtz has also been a visiting critic and juror at Columbia University.

MARK MARKIEWICZ

AIA

Mark Markiewicz earned his Bachelor of Arts and Master of Architecture degrees from Princeton University in 1972 and 1974 respectively. He joined Mitchell/Giurgola in 1975 and was named an associate of the firm in 1981 and a partner in 1986.

Mr Markiewicz is concerned with the broad range of design, from the conceptual initiation of master plans through to detail design. His projects include those of civic scale as well as those of more intimate dimensions. He has collaborated with artists including Valerie Jaudon, Jennifer Bartlett, and Lin Utzon to integrate their commissions with building projects.

His drawings for "Building by Design: Architecture at IBM" were exhibited at the National Building Museum. He also brings to the firm's projects a strong sensibility and interest in the issues of interior design, including custom carpets and furniture.

Mr Markiewicz has been a visiting critic and juror at Columbia University (1983–present) and Parsons School of Design (1984–present), as well as at Barnard College and Princeton University. In addition, he has been an active contributor to the profession through his work with the New York City Chapter of the American Institute of Architects. He is a member of the Design Awards Committee (1988–present) and former Chairman of the Committee (1992–93).

Mr Markiewicz is the author, with Paul Broches, of "Learning in Luxury, The New IBM Advanced Business Institute," *Interspace 91*; and a contributor to the exhibition catalogue, *Window, Room, Furniture,* a Cooper Union Publication.

Collaborating Partners
Selected and Current Works 1986–1996

MEETING PLACES

Project	Collaborating Partners
Anchorage Historical and Fine Arts Museum	Steven Goldberg Romaldo Giurgola
Advanced Business Institute, IBM Corporation	Paul Broches Mark Markiewicz Romaldo Giurgola Dart Sageser
Virginia Air and Space Center/ Hampton Roads History Center	Steven Goldberg John Kurtz Romaldo Giurgola
Fine and Performing Arts Center, University of West Florida	Steven Goldberg Mark Markiewicz
Onondaga County Convention Center	Steven Goldberg Mark Markiewicz Dart Sageser
Harlem International Trade Center	Steven Goldberg Jan Keane Mark Markiewicz

RESEARCH/STUDY PLACES

Project	Collaborating Partners
George M. Low Center for Industrial Innovation, Rensselaer Polytechnic Institute	Jan Keane Romaldo Giurgola
Outpatient Care Center, University of California at Los Angeles	Mark Markiewicz Romaldo Giurgola Dart Sageser
Revelle College Sciences Building, University of California at San Diego	Mark Markiewicz Randall Leach
Life Sciences Building, Ciba Pharmaceuticals	Jan Keane John Kurtz Romaldo Giurgola
Ceramics Corridor Innovation Center, Corning	Jan Keane John Kurtz
Ceramics Corridor Innovation Center, Alfred	Jan Keane John Kurtz
Stafford Hall, Microbiology/Orthopaedics Research Building, University of Vermont	Jan Keane John Kurtz
Laboratory Science Building, College of Staten Island	Paul Broches Mark Markiewicz

Metcalfe Student Center, Long Island University	Paul Broches John Kurtz
Zeckendorf Health Sciences Center, Long Island University	Paul Broches John Kurtz
Administrative and Student Services Building, Hostos Community College	Paul Broches Mark Markiewicz
PS 88, The Seneca School	Paul Broches John Kurtz
PS 56, Richmond Elementary School	Paul Broches John Kurtz

WORK PLACES

Project	Collaborating Partners
Volvo Corporate Headquarters	Mark Markiewicz Romaldo Giurgola Dart Sageser
300 Atlantic Street Office Building	Steven Goldberg Romaldo Giurgola
Center West, Office/Retail/Parking	Paul Broches Steven Goldberg Romaldo Giurgola
Solana Office/Parking Complex, IBM Corporation/Maguire Thomas Partners	Paul Broches Jan Keane John Kurtz Romaldo Giurgola
Columbus Center	Paul Broches Mark Markiewicz
The Lighthouse Inc. Headquarters	Steven Goldberg Jan Keane John Kurtz Mark Markiewicz

PUBLIC SPACES/PLACES

Project	Collaborating Partners
Hudson View East Residential Development	Steven Goldberg Randall Leach
Davenport Downtown Plan and River Center Plaza	Paul Broches
Intertech Corporation, Office Development Master Plan	Steven Goldberg Jan Keane
St Joseph's College Comprehensive Plan	Paul Broches
Southampton College Master Plan	Paul Broches
The Belvedere, Battery Park City	Steven Goldberg John Kurtz

Chronological List of Selected Buildings & Projects

* Indicates work featured in this book
(see Selected and Current Works)

Selected Projects prior to 1986

Dayton Residence
Wayzata, Minnesota
1970

Mission Park Residential Houses
Williams College
Williamstown, Massachusetts
1972

Office and Assembly Building
US Car Manufacturing Division
Volvo of America Corporation
Chesapeake, Virginia
1976

Sherman Fairchild Center for the Life Sciences
Columbia University
New York, New York
1977

Competition Entry for a New Parliament House
Canberra, Australia
1979

Newman Residence
Bedford, New York
1979

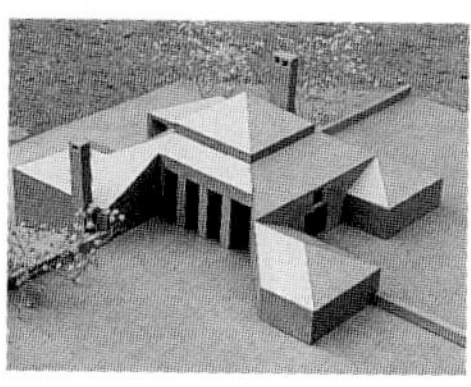

Elementary School
Associazione Nationale Alpini
US Agency for International Development
Aviano, Italy
1981

Student Housing
Associazione Nationale Alpini
US Agency for International Development
San Pietro al Natisone, Italy
1981

Technical High School
Associazione Nationale Alpini
US Agency for International Development
Maniago, Italy
1981

US Capitol Grounds Master Plan
Washington, DC
1981

Health Services Building, College of Health Sciences, Technology and Management Building
Massachusetts Institute of Technology
Cambridge, Massachusetts
With Gruzen & Partners
1982

Wainwright State Office Complex
State of Missouri
St Louis, Missouri
With Hastings and Chivetta, Architects
1982

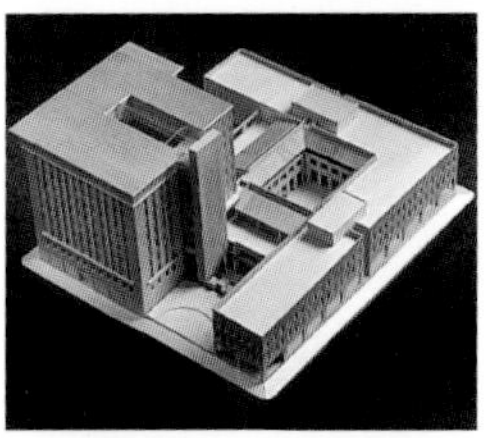

Burke Library Renovation
Union Theological Seminary
New York, New York
1983

Westlake Park Master Plan
IBM Corporation
Westlake, Texas
1984

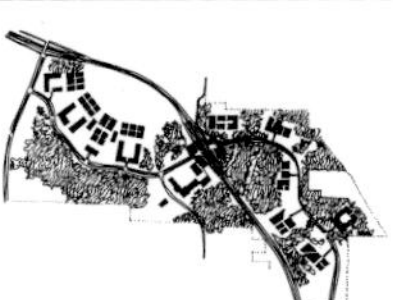

***Anchorage Historical and Fine Arts Museum**
Municipality of Anchorage
Anchorage, Alaska
With Maynard and Partch, Architects
1985

***Volvo Corporate Headquarters**
AB Volvo Corporation
Gothenburg, Sweden
With Owe Svard, Architect
1985

***Davenport Downtown Plan and River Center Plaza**
City of Davenport and Visiting Artists, Inc.
Davenport, Iowa
1986

***George M. Low Center for Industrial Innovation**
Rensselaer Polytechnic Institute
Troy, New York
1987

***Hudson View East Residential Development**
The Zeckendorf Company
New York, New York
1987

***Advanced Business Institute**
IBM Corporation
Palisades, New York
1989

***Solana Office/Parking Complex**
IBM Corporation and Maguire Thomas Partners
Westlake/Southlake, Texas
1989

***Center West, Office/Retail/Parking**
Center West
Los Angeles, California
With Daniel, Mann, Johnson & Mendenhall
1990

***Intertech Corporation, Office Development Master Plan**
Louden, Virginia
1990

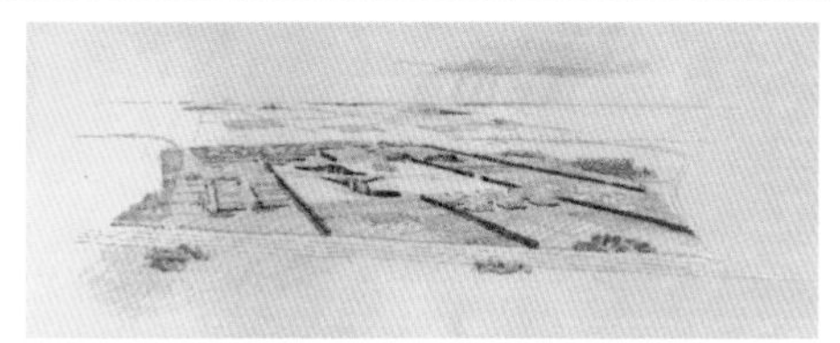

***Outpatient Care Center**
University of California at Los Angeles
Los Angeles, California
With Daniel, Mann, Johnson & Mendenhall
1990

***300 Atlantic Street Office Building**
F.D. Rich Company
Stamford, Connecticut
1990

***Columbus Center**
Coral Gables Associates
Coral Gables, Florida
With The Nichols Partnership
1991

***Ceramics Corridor Innovation Center**
Alfred Technology Resources/New York State Urban Development Corporation
Corning, New York
1992

***Ceramics Corridor Innovation Center**
Alfred Technology Resources/New York State Urban Development Corporation
Alfred, New York
1992

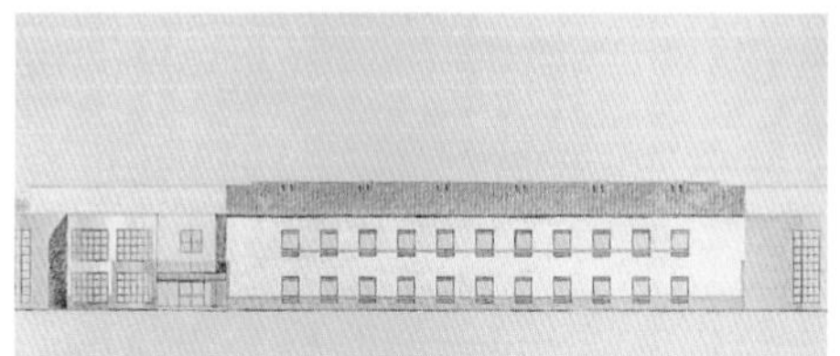

***Fine and Performing Arts Center**
University of West Florida
Pensacola, Florida
With Barrett, Daffin and Carlan, Inc.
1992

***Onondaga County Convention Center**
County of Onondaga/New York State Urban Development Corporation
Syracuse, New York
1992

***Virginia Air and Space Center/Hampton Roads History Center**
City of Hampton
Hampton, Virginia
With Rancorn, Wildman, Krause Brezinski
1992

***Revelle College Sciences Building**
University of California at San Diego
LaJolla, California
With Austin Hansen Fehlman Architects
1993

***Stafford Hall, Microbiology/Orthopaedics Research Building**
University of Vermont
Burlington, Vermont
1993

***St Joseph's College Comprehensive Plan**
Patchogue, New York
1994

***Southampton College Master Plan**
Long Island University
Southampton, New York
1994

***Life Sciences Building**
Ciba Pharmaceuticals
Summit, New Jersey
1994

***The Lighthouse Inc. Headquarters**
The Lighthouse Inc.
New York, New York
1994

***The Belvedere**
Battery Park City Authority
New York, New York
With Child Associates Inc.
1995

***Laboratory Science Building**
College of Staten Island
City University of New York
Staten Island, New York
1995

***Metcalfe Student Center**
Long Island University,
Brooklyn Campus
Brooklyn, New York
1995

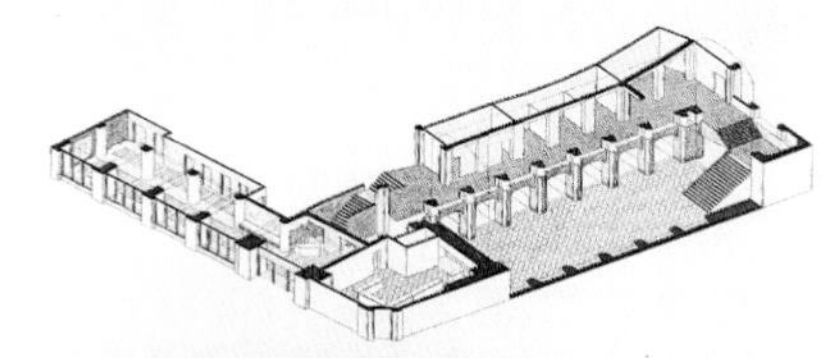

***Zeckendorf Health Sciences Center**
Long Island University,
Brooklyn Campus
Brooklyn, New York
1995

***PS 88, The Seneca School**
New York City School Construction
Authority
Queens, New York
1996

***Administrative and Student Services Building**
Hostos Community College,
The City University of New York
Bronx, New York
1997

***PS 56, Richmond Elementary School**
New York City School Construction
Authority
Staten Island, New York
1997

***Harlem International Trade Center**
Harlem International Trade Center
Corporation/New York State Urban
Development Corporation
Harlem, New York
With Roberta Washington, Architect
1998

Selected Design Awards

National Honor Award for Urban Design
The American Institute of Architects
The Belvedere
Battery Park City Authority
New York, New York
1996

National Award for Excellence in Universal Design
National Building Museum and National Endowment for the Arts
Lighthouse National Headquarters
The Lighthouse Inc.
New York, New York
1996

National Honor Award for Interiors
The American Institute of Architects
Lighthouse National Headquarters
The Lighthouse Inc.
New York, New York
1996

International Award for Excellence on the Waterfront
The Waterfront Center
The Belvedere
Battery Park City Authority
New York, New York
1995

Access New York Award
Manhattan Borough President's Office
Lighthouse National Headquarters
The Lighthouse Inc.
New York, New York
1995

Access New York Award
Manhattan Borough President's Office
Community Church Entrance Pavilion
New York, New York
1995

INFORM Interiors Award
The Virginia Society/AIA
Virginia Air & Space Center/Hampton Roads History Center
Hampton, Virginia
1995

1995 Lab of the Year Award
R & D Magazine
CIBA-Geigy Life Sciences Building
Summit, New Jersey
1995

The New Good Neighbor Award
New Jersey Business Council
CIBA-Geigy Life Sciences Building
Summit, New Jersey
1995

Insight Award
Society of Environmental Graphic Designers
Lighthouse National Headquarters
The Lighthouse Inc.
New York, New York
1994

Grand Award Winner
IX Panamerican Biennial for Architecture
College of Architects of Ecuador
Virginia Air & Space Center/Hampton Roads History Center
Hampton, Virginia
1994

Grand Award Winner
Concrete Awards Committee
New Jersey Chapter/ACI and New Jersey Concrete and Aggregate Association
CIBA-Geigy Life Sciences Building
Summit, New Jersey
1994

Juror's Award
Society for Environmental Graphic Design
Virginia Air & Space Center/Hampton Roads History Center
Hampton, Virginia
1993

Governmental Construction Category Design Award
Virginia Masonry Council
Hampton Parking Facility
Hampton, Virginia
1993

Excellence in Architecture with Honor
The Virginia Society/AIA
Virginia Air & Space Center/Hampton Roads History Center
Hampton, Virginia
1992

Harry H. Edwards Industry Advancement Award
Precast/Prestressed Concrete Institute
CIBA-Geigy Life Sciences Building
Summit, New Jersey
1992

Certificate of Design Excellence
Print Casebooks 9
Phase I, IBM Office/Parking Complex, Solana
Westlake/Southlake, Texas
1992

Citation for Excellence
New York Chapter/AIA
Phase I, IBM Office/Parking Complex, Solana
Westlake/Southlake, Texas
1991

Beautification Award Finalist
New Commercial High Rise Category
Los Angeles Business Council
Center West, Office/Retail/Parking
Los Angeles, California
1991

Beautification Award
Public Use/Public Interior Category
Los Angeles Business Council
Center West, Office/Retail/Parking
Los Angeles, California
1991

Citation for Excellence
New York Chapter/AIA
Advanced Business Institute, IBM
Palisades, New York
1991

First Honor Award
Community Design Award Program
Westchester/Mid-Hudson Chapter/AIA
Advanced Business Institute, IBM
Palisades, New York
1990

Merit Award
The American Society of Landscape Architects
Phase I, IBM Office/Parking Complex, Solana
Westlake/Southlake, Texas
1989

Honor Award
Alaska Chapter/AIA
Anchorage Historical and Fine Arts Museum
Anchorage, Alaska
1986

Winning Submission
Tallahassee-Leon County Civic Center
Competition
Tallahassee, Florida
1986

National Honor Award
The American Institute of Architects
Corporate Headquarters, AB Volvo
Gothenburg, Sweden
1985

Distinguished Architecture Award
New York Chapter/AIA
Corporate Headquarters, AB Volvo
Gothenburg, Sweden
1985

Distinguished Architecture Award
New York Chapter/AIA
Aviano Elementary School
Aviano, Italy
1984

Distinguished Architecture Award
New York Chapter/AIA
The Burke Library Renovation
Union Theological Seminary
New York, New York
1984

Excellence in Design Award
New York State Association of Architects
Aviano Elementary School
Aviano, Italy
1983

Build Massachusetts Award
Associated General Contractors of Massachusetts
Health Services Center and Whitaker College of Health Sciences, Technology, and Management, Massachusetts Institute of Technology
Cambridge, Massachusetts
1982

Excellence in Design Award
New York State Association of Architects
Tilles Center for Performing Arts (Bush-Brown Concert Theater), C.W. Post Center
Long Island University
Greenvale, New York
1982

Silver Medal, First Design Award
Pennsylvania Society of Architects
Wainwright State Office Complex
St Louis, Missouri
1981

Winning Submission
Parliament House Australia Competition
Canberra, Australia
1980

Excellence in Design Award
New York State Association of Architects
Benjamin F. Feinberg Library
State University of New York, College at Plattsburgh
Plattsburgh, New York
1979

Honor Award
Philadelphia Chapter/AIA
Benjamin F. Feinberg Library
State University of New York, College at Plattsburgh
Plattsburgh, New York
1979

Gold Medal, First Design Award
Philadelphia Chapter/AIA
Sherman Fairchild Center for the Life Sciences, Columbia University
New York, New York
1979

Citation
Progressive Architecture
Westlake Park
Seattle, Washington
1978

Design Award
Urban Design
Westlake Park
Seattle, Washington
1978

Bard Award for Excellence
The City Club of New York
Sherman Fairchild Center for the Life Sciences, Columbia University
New York, New York
1978

Architectural Firm Award
The American Institute of Architects
1976

Medal of Honor, Firm Award
New York City Chapter/AIA
1975

Landmark Preservation Award
Design & Environment
Wainwright State Office Complex Competition
St Louis, Missouri
1975

Silver Medal, First Design Award
Pennsylvania Society of Architects
Student Union, State University of New York, College at Plattsburgh
Plattsburgh, New York
1975

Winning Submission
Wainwright State Office Complex Competition
St Louis, Missouri
1974

Honorable Mention
New York State Association of Architects
Student Union, State University of New York, College at Plattsburgh
Plattsburgh, New York
1974

Bibliography

General Writing on the Firm

Broches, Paul. "La arquitectura de comunida agradable." *TRAMA: Revista de Arquitectura* (December 1994).

Dattner, Richard. *Civil Architecture: The New Public Infrastructure.* New York: McGraw-Hill Inc., 1995.

Laseau, Paul. *Architectural Drawing: Options for Design.* Design Press, 1991.

Mitchell/Giurgola Architects. Forward by Kenneth Frampton, New York: Rizzoli International Publications Inc., 1983.

Mitchell/Giurgola Architects, *Space Design* (Special feature, Japan, August, 1986).

Rykwert, Joseph. "Mitchell/Giurgola Profile (1978–1988)." *Process: Architecture No. 81* (Tokyo, March 1989).

Sommer, Degenhard (ed.). *Industriebau: Europa, Japan, USA,* (Praxis Report). Contributors: John Loomis, Malcolm S. Whyte. Basel: Birkhauser Verlag AG, 1991.

Vreeland, Thomas R. Jr, Victor A. Lundy, Paul Heyer & Ulrich Franzen. "Mitchell/Giurgola Profile (1958–1978)." *Process: Architecture No. 2* (Tokyo, 1977). Interview by Ching Yu-Chang.

Wilkes, Joseph A. (ed.). *The Encyclopedia of Architecture.* New York: John Wiley and Sons Inc./American Institute of Architects, 1989.

World of Today's Architecture & Design. Barcelona, Spain: Links International, 1996.

Individual Projects

300 Atlantic Street Office Building

Corporate Design & Realty (May 1986).

New York Times (Real Estate section, March 2, 1986).

Administrative and Student Services Building, Hostos Community College

Richards, Kristen. "Dreams Do Come True." *Interiors* (November, 1994), pp. 20–7.

Advanced Business Institute, IBM Corporation

Baumeister (December 1988).

Gardner, Carl (ed.). *Interspace 1991: The International Review of Contract Interior Design and Architecture.* London: Sterling Publications International Limited, 1991.

Knight, Carleton III. "Clients: IBM Returns to Its Roots." *Architecture* (June 1986).

Pearson, Clifford. "An Honorable Retreat." *Architectural Record* (September 1989).

Penner, Richard H. *Conference Center Planning and Design: A Guide for Architects, Designers, Meeting Planners, and Facility Managers.* New York: Restaurant/Hotel Design International/Whitney Library of Design/Watson-Guptill Publications, 1991.

Anchorage Historical and Fine Arts Museum

"Dignified Simplicity in a Mighty Landscape." *Architectural Record* (April 1986).

Goldberg, Steven M. "Light & Architecture Enhance Communication with Art." *Lighting Design + Application* (July 1986).

Northwest Arts: Fortnightly Journal of News and Opinion (vol. XII, no. 15, August 22, 1986).

Shalkop, Robert & Steven M. Goldberg. "Northern Light in a Museum." *Museum News* (April 1987).

Aviano Elementary School, Maniago Technical High School

"Aviano Elementary School, Italy, Maniago Technical High School, Italy." *Baumeister* (March 1988).

The Belvedere, Battery Park City

Construction Data News (vol. 19, no. 52, September 11, 1995).

Dunlap, David W. "Opening New Fronts at Battery Park City." *New York Times* (Real Estate section, September 4, 1994).

International Architecture Yearbook, Volume 2. Melbourne, Australia: The Images Publishing Group, 1996. pp. 294–295.

Landecker, Heidi. "Waterfront Connection." *Architecture* (August 1995), pp. 56–61.

Melrod, George. "Skill, Vision, and Craft: Martin Puryear Lets His Sculpture Speak For Itself." *Art & Antiques,* (June 1995) pp. 39–43.

World of Today's Architecture & Design. Barcelona, Spain: Links International, 1996.

Casa Manana Theatre

Gay, Wayne Lee. "Change of Venue." *Fort Worth Star-Telegram* (March 8, 1990).

Center West, Office/Retail/Parking

Davis, Carlton. "Center West: Gateway to Westwood?" *LA Architect* (April 1990).

Designer West (February 1991).

Sachner, Paul M. "Good Taste." *Architectural Record* (October 1990).

Columbus Center

Dunlop, Beth. "Columbus Center Sets a Bold New Standard." *Miami Herald* (Science section, May 19, 1991).

"On The Boards." *Architecture* (December 1990).

"Project Seeks to Preserve City Style." *Miami Herald* (Commercial Real Estate section, March 19, 1990).

Fine and Performing Arts Center, University of West Florida

"Art Imitates Animals at U. of West Florida." *Chronicle of Higher Education* (November 23, 1994), p. A5.

Franklin Delano Roosevelt Memorial Park Update and Southpoint Sea Walls

Walton, Thomas. "Renewing the Mandate for Design Excellence in America's Public Realm." *Places: A Forum of Environmental Design* (vol. 9, no. 2, Summer 1994).

George M. Low Center for Industrial Innovation, Rensselaer Polytechnic Institute

"In the Northeast." *Architectural Record* (July 1987).

Lloyd, Holly & Lee Ingalls (eds). *University Science Facilities: 100 Project Profiles.* Orinda, CA: Tradeline Publications, 1993, p. 86.

Harlem International Trade Center

Kennedy, Shawn G. "Harlem Dreams Are Revived for Trade Center and Hotel." *New York Times* (Metro section, November 14, 1994).

Hudson View East Residential Development

"Battery Park City Update." *Progressive Architecture* (June 1986).

"Building the New City." *Progressive Architecture* (March 1988).

"On High-Rise Residences." *Process: Architecture No. 64* (January 1986).

Laboratory Science Building, College of Staten Island

"Laboratory Science Building to Service Many Departments from Two Campuses." *New York Construction News* (August 28, 1995).

Life Sciences Building, Ciba Pharmaceuticals

"Ciba-Geigy's Life Sciences Building." *Facilities Planning News* (vol. 12, no. 3, March 1993).

Crosbie, Michael J. "Machines for Discovery." *Progressive Architecture* (November 1994), pp. 62–63.

ENR (Engineering News Record) (December 2, 1991).

International Architecture Yearbook, Volume 1, Book 1. Melbourne, Australia: The Images Publishing Group, 1995, pp. 24–7.

"Interstitial Prestressed Concrete Trusses Featured in CIBA-Geigy Laboratory Building." *PCI Journal* (June 1992).

"Lab Profits From Interstitial Solution." *Building Design & Construction* (September 1995), pp. 32–6.

"Laboratory of the Year." *R&D Magazine* (May 1995), pp. 34–7.

L'industria Italiana del Cemento (Rome, Italy, Fall 1995).

Levy, Matthys P. & Tony Yoshizawa. "Interstitial Precast Prestressed Concrete Trusses for CIBA-Geigy Life Science Building." *PCI Journal* (November/December 1992).

The Lighthouse Inc. Headquarters

Bosco, Pearl. "The ADA: Today, Tomorrow, and Tomorrow?" *Buildings* (April 1994).

Covington, George & Bruce Hannah. *Access By Design.* New York: Van Nostrand-Reinhold, 1996.

Geran, Monica. "The Lighthouse, Mitchell/Giurgola." *Interior Design* (August 1995), pp. 80–7.

Goldberg, Steven (ed.), *The Lighthouse Headquarters, New York: A National Model for People with Impaired Vision,* Neocon Whitepaper, June 1994.

International Architecture Yearbook, Volume 2. Melbourne, Australia: The Images Publishing Group, 1996. pp. 220–223.

New York Times (Real Estate section, March 3, 1991).

Otake, Hideko. "News from New York." *Tostem View* (vol. 54, July 1995), p. 15.

Rosenfeld, Erika. "The Lighthouse: A Beacon of Sensitive, Sensible Design." *AIArchitect* (Affiliate News, January 1995), p. 21.

Rumble, Janet L. "Lighting the Way." *Metropolis* (April 1995), pp. 71–105.

Schmertz, Mildred. "Community Beacon." *Architecture* (June 1995), pp. 94–101.

Slatin, Peter D. "Lighthouse for the Blind Manhattan Headquarters, New York." *Architectural Record Houses* (no. 4, 1991).

Slatin, Peter. "Beyond Wheelchairs." *Architectural Record* (August 1993).

Slatin, Peter. "Darkness Made Visible." *Interior Design* (September/October 1993).

Slatin, Peter. "The Lighthouse Gets Bright, Airy New Headquarters." *New York Times* (Real Estate section, June 19, 1994).

"Universal Design at the Lighthouse." *Facilities Design and Management* (May 1994).

World of Today's Architecture & Design. Barcelona, Spain: Links International, 1996.

Metcalfe Student Center, Long Island University

"A New Building for LIU." *New York Times* (Real Estate section, October 1, 1995).

Gray, Christopher. "Once a Rococo Palace, Now a Citadel of Learning." *New York Times* (Real Estate section, July 31, 1994).

MIT Health Services and Whitaker College of Health Sciences, Technology and Management

Sageser, Dart with Sarah Shankman. "A Marriage of Form and Function, Research and Application." *Lighting Design + Application* (July 1987).

Onondaga County Convention Center

"Onondaga County Convention Center, Syracuse, New York." *Architecture Now, A visual Survey of Current Projects From the World's Premier Architects.* Volume One. Tokyo, Japan: Sigma Union, Inc., 1994.

Outpatient Care Center, University of California at Los Angeles

Landecker, Heidi. "Campus Cure." *Architecture* (July 1991).

Stocker, Lori J.P. "Reflective Glass in the UCLA Medical Center." *US Glass, Metal & Glazing* (August 1992).

Revelle College Sciences Building, University of California at San Diego

"Imported Ingenuity." *Architecture* (May 1990).

International Architecture Yearbook, Volume 1, Book 1. Melbourne, Australia: The Images Publishing Group, 1995, pp. 84–7.

Lloyd, Holly & Lee Ingalls (eds). *University Science Facilities: 100 Project Profiles.* Orinda, CA: Tradeline Publications, 1993, p. 144.

Solana Office/Parking Complex, IBM Corporation/Maguire Thomas Partners

"1988 ASLA Awards." *Landscape Architecture* (November 1988).

"A Remarkable Place in the Sun." *Southern Accents* (February 1991).

Barna, Joel W. "Solana in the Sun." *Progressive Architecture* (April 1989).

Baumeister (April 1990).

Dillon, David. "Corporate Villas." *Landscape Architect* (March 1990).

Dillon, David. "IBM's Colorful 'Place in the Sun'." *Architecture* (May 1989).

Dillon, David. *Dallas Morning News* (Arts section, October 9, 1988).

Goldberger, Paul. "IBM's Urbane New Place in the Sun in Texas." *New York Times* (October 22, 1989).

Interior Design (August 1989).

Lawrence, John F. "Nice Profits from Better City Life." *Fortune* (October 9, 1989).

Posner, Ellen. "Architecture: Visiting Solana." *Wall Street Journal* (November 8, 1989).

Progressive Architecture (news report, July 1986).

Winters, Willis. "If You Build It, They Will Come." *Texas Architect* (vol. 3, no. 4, 1992).

Sports and Recreation Facility, Southampton College, Long Island University

Freedman, Mitchell. "Pooling Their Resources: LIU and Southampton Trying to Get Locals in the Swim." *Newsday* (December 11, 1994).

Love, Douglas P. "LIU Seeks Town Help To Build Rink and Pool." *Southampton Press* (November 24, 1994).

Virginia Air and Space Center/Hampton Roads History Center

"Air and Space Center Proves Tough to Land." *ENR (Engineering News Record)* (March 4, 1991).

"Air and Water Mix at Award Winning Museum by Mitchell/Giurgola." *Architectural Record* (Design News, February 1995), p. 15.

"Cool Storage Case Study." *Virginia Power* (Fall 1992).

Abitare (June 1993).

Architectural Record (Design News, May 1988).

Barhydt, Matthew. *Oculus* (March 1995), p. 3.

Cunningham, Aimee. "Flight of Fancy." *inform: architecture-design-the arts* (vol. 3, no. 4, Fall 1992).

Dugger, Keli. "From the Sea to the Stars." *Designers West* (November 1992).

International Yearbook of Prizewinning Architecture, 1995. Cologne, Germany: Architektur Optimal, 1995.

Landecker, Heidi. "Hampton Takes Flight." *Architecture* (September 1992).

Maurer, Richard. "Virginia Air, Space, History Center: A Happy Marriage." *Exhibit Builder* (March/April 1993).

"Virginia Air & Space Center/Hampton Roads History Center, Hampton, Virginia." *Architecture Now: A Visual Survey of Current Projects from the World's Premier Architects.* Volume Two. Tokyo, Japan: Sigma Union, Inc., 1994.

"'Winged' Structure to House Air and Space Museum." *Building Design and Construction* (January 1991).

Volvo Corporate Headquarters

Bauwelt (no. 13, April 4, 1986).

"Artist + Architect + Corporation." *Art & Auction* (November 1986).

Wainwright State Office Building

Kultermann, Prof. Udo. "Glas als Brucke zwischen alt und neu." *Architektur* (no. 8, 1991).

Zeckendorf Health Sciences Center

"A New Building for LIU." *New York Times* (Real Estate section, October 1, 1995).

Construction News (vol. XLI, no. 31, March 14, 1994).

Negron, Edna. "Laboratories in Demand." *Newsday* (November 12, 1993).

Acknowledgments

Successful projects are the result of successful collaborations between the design team and an enlightened client. We are particularly grateful to each of our clients. They have sustained the firm and its goals.

Internally, the firm depends on its professional staff for the success of its projects. Design teams established at the outset of every commission work closely together with one or several partners and associates for the duration of the project. This assures a systematic development of the design and implementation process that is consistent with the architects' intentions.

In appreciation for the extraordinary contribution of the Mitchell/Giurgola staff, below are listed those individuals who have been with the firm for all or part of the ten-year period covered by the work in this book. Special appreciation is given to the associates who have provided exceptional leadership and support.

Finally we extend our appreciation to Christa Mahar for her great skill, dedication, and valiant efforts to assemble the materials for this monograph. Her close working relationship with the publisher was invaluable.

Associates

James Braddock
Margaret W. DeBolt
Carol Loewenson
Susan Stando

Staff

Kathy Achepohl
Amy Anderson
Clif Balch
David Beem
Sergei Bischak
David Bogle
Lisa Borgmeier
Agnete Bryndorf
Niall Cain
Fred Chung
Melissa Cicetti
Ann Cleary
Brad Cloepfil
Timothy Costello
Stuart Crawford
Mark Devlin
Stephen Dietz
Pamela Dragonetti
Steve Dumas
David Esch
Henry Ferretti
Shannon Fowler
Joshua Frankel
David Fratianne
Tilman Globig
Mark Gordon
Ed Harrington
Tony Hartin
Laura Heim
Roisin Heneghan
Simo Hoite
Donald Hunsicker
Brian Jonas
Michelle Kayon
Cristal Knappe
Joseph Lengeling
Richard Lew
Mary Elizabeth Liggio
John Loomis
Taylor Louden
Thomas Lurcott
Christa Mahar
Daniel Maney
Michael Manfredi
Andrew Mazor
Jylle Menoff
Ursula Emery McClure
Leslie Neblett
Randall Ott
Stefano Paci
Jon Paddock
Alexandra Papageorgiou
Amy Philips
Scott Phillips
Robert Pils
Sarah Purcell
Frank Rascoe
Channing Redford
Miguel Rivera
Joanne Robinson
Kathy Sachar
Rebecca Schneier
Michael Selditch
Kelly Shannon
Brad Sick
David Taber
Mark Thometz
Craig Tooman
Jose Toro
Gabriel Toyos
Malka van Bemmelen
Charles Wahl
Robert Weir
Marion Weiss

Past Partners and Associates

Romaldo Giurgola
Nancy Brandenburg
Randall Leach
Dart Sageser

In addition, each project is the result of the efforts of many specialists.
In particular, we would like to acknowledge the insight and collaborative contributions of the following consultants.

Mechanical/Electrical/ Plumbing Engineers

Atkinson Koven & Feinberg

Cosentini Associates

DVL Consulting Engineers, Inc.

Earl Walls Associates

Flack + Kurtz Consulting Engineers, LLP

Hardie & Associates

H.C. Yu and Associates

Jaros, Baum & Bolles

Joseph R. Loring Associates

Kallen and Lemelson

Lehr Associates, Consulting Engineers

Lakhani & Jordan Engineers

Mariano D. Molina, Consulting Engineers

Newcomb & Boyd

Syska & Hennessey

Structural and Civil Engineers

Durbrow Associates

Ewell Finley and Partners, Inc.

John P. Stopen Engineering Partnership

Langan Engineering and Environmental Services

Leslie E. Robertson & Associates

Ove Arup & Partners

Salmon Associates

Severud Associates

Weidlinger Associates

Ysrael A. Seinuk, P.C. Consulting Engineers

Landscape Architects

Child Associates Inc. Landscape Architects

Lois Sherr, Landscape Architects

Michael Van Valkenburgh Associates, Inc.

Michel & Associates

Peter Walker & Martha Schwartz

Rolland/Towers Landscape Architects

Thomas Balsley Associates

Cost Consultants

Federman Design and Construction Consultants

M.T. Peters & Associates

VJ Associates

Wolf & Company

Specialty Consultants

Ann Kale Associates

Cerami & Associates

Cini-Little International

Donnell Consultants, Inc.

Fisher Dachs Associates

Fisher Marantz Renfro Stone

Grid Properties, Inc.

H.M. Brandston & Partners

Jaffe Holden Scarbrough Acoustics

John A. Van Deusen & Associates, Inc.

Kirkegaard & Associates

Krent/Paffett Associates, Inc.

Robert A. Hansen Associates

Rolf Jensen & Associates

Romano Gatland

Shen Milsom & Wilke

Superstructures

Vincent Ciulla

Whitehouse & Company

Woodward Clyde Consultants

General Contractors/ Construction Managers

AFC Enterprises, Inc.

ASC Construction

Barr & Barr

Cowper Construction Company

F.D. Rich Construction Company, Inc.

F.O. Petersson

Granger Northern, Inc.

Hardin Construction Group, Inc.

HCB Contractors

Held Jones

HRH Construction Corporation

Huber Hunt & Nichols, Inc.

Indus Corporation

Interstate Company, Inc.

Ken Brady Construction Company Inc.

Keuka Construction Corporation

Lease Kissee Construction Co.

Lehrer McGovern Bovis

McCarthy Western Constructors

McGuire & Bennett

Peck/Jones Brothers

Raytheon Engineers & Constructors

TDX Construction Corporation

Torcon, Inc.

Whiting-Turner Contracting Company

W.M. Jordan Company, Inc.

York Hunter Inc.

Photo Credits

Without the co-operation and support of Esto Photographics, the publication of this monograph would not be possible. We would like to acknowledge the fine work of these professionals and their permission to reproduce the images in this collection.

David Michael Bernard: 17 (lower right); 54 (2); 56 (6); 57 (7,8); 58 (10); 59 (11,12).

Craig Blackmon/BlackmonWinters: 3 (upper right); 145 (upper left).

Tom Bonner: 87 (2,3); 89 (7).

Paul Broches: 136 (1); 192 (10).

Elio Ciol: 242 (a–c).

Tom Crane: 37 (14); 38 (16); 40 (20); 42 (25).

Mark Darley/Esto: 184 (18).

Robert I. Faulkner: 103 (10); 104 (11); 106 (17); 107 (20).

Scott Frances/Esto: front cover; 78 (2); 79 (3); 80 (5); 81 (7); 83 (10,11); 84 (13); 86 (9); 88 (5); 90 (9); 91 (10); 108 (2); 109 (3,4); 110 (6,7); 111 (8,9); 112 (2); 113 (3); 114 (6,7); 115 (8–10); 145 (upper right, lower right); 161 (3,4); 162 (5); 163 (6); 164 (7,8); 165 (9,10); 166 (2); 167 (3); 168 (4); 169 (5); 170 (7); 171 (8,9); 172 (10); 173 (11); 243 (d,h); 244 (e).

Jeff Goldberg/Esto: inside sleeve; 3 (upper left, lower right); 11 (lower); 12 (lower); 13 (upper); 14 (left, right); 17 (upper left); 44 (2); 45 (3); 46 (5); 47 (6); 48 (7–9); 49 (10,11); 50 (12,13); 51 (16,17); 52 (18); 53 (19); 60 (2); 61 (4); 62 (5,6); 64 (10); 65 (11,12); 66 (13); 68 (15,16); 69 (17); 71 (20); 77 (upper right, lower left, lower right); 98 (2); 99 (3); 100 (4); 101 (5–7); 104 (12); 105 (13,14); 106 (16); 107 (19); 117 (2,3); 118 (4–6); 119 (7,8); 120 (12); 121 (13–15); 122 (16,17); 123 (18,19); 124 (1); 125 (3); 127 (8–10); 128 (2); 129 (3); 130 (2); 131 (3); 132 (4–6); 133 (7–9); 134 (12,13); 135 (14–16); 197 (3); 198 (4); 199 (5–7); 200 (9,10); 201 (11,14); 202 (15); 203 (16); 204 (17,18); 205 (19,20); 206 (24); 207 (25–28); 209 (bottom right); 210 (2); 211 (3); 212 (4,5); 213 (7); 223 (3); 224 (4,5); 225 (6,7); 226 (9); 227 (11,12); 228 (14); 229 (15–18); 243 (e); (244 (h,i); 245 (b,e,f,g); 246 (b).

Tim Griffith (photographer The Images Publishing Group)/Jody Dole (computer retoucher): 61 (4).

Tim Griffith/The Images Publishing Group: 63 (7); 67 (14).

Mick Hales: 10 (upper); 17 (lower left); 33 (7); 31 (3,4); 32 (5,6); 33 (7); 35 (10–12); 36 (13); 38 (15); 39 (17,18); 40 (19); 41 (21,22); 42 (23,24); 43 (26–28); 243 (f).

Jim Hedrich/Hedrich-Blessing: 179 (10); 180 (11); 181 (12); 193 (12).

Keld Helmer-Peterson: 8; 15; 145 (lower left); 146 (2); 147 (4); 148 (7); 149 (10); 150 (12); 151 (13,14); 152 (15,16); 153 (18–20); 154 (20,21); 155 (22,23); 156 (24–26); 157 (27); 158 (28–30); 159 (31).

David Hewitt/Anne Garrison: 3 (lower left); 77 (upper left); 93 (3,4); 94 (6); 95 (7,8); 96 (10); 97 (11–13); 245 (a).

Rollin R La France 241 (a,b); 242 (f).

Marco Lorenzetti/Hedrich-Blessing: 186 (2); 187 (3); 188 (5); 189 (6); 191 (9); 193 (11–13); 194 (14); 195 (15).

Norman McGrath: 242 (g).

Richard Payne: 174 (2); 175 (3); 178 (9); 182 (14,15); 183 (16); 184 (17); 243 (g).

Jock Pottle/Esto: 73 (3); 74 (6); 75 (9); 92 (2); 137 (3–5); 140 (2); 141 (3); 212 (4,6).

Steven Rosenthal: 242 (e).

Guy Sussman: 241 (c,d).

Wesley L. Thompson: 185 (19).

Paul Warchol: 9 (upper, lower); 17 (upper right); 18 (2); 19 (3,4); 20 (5); 21 (8,9); 24 (14,15); 25 (16–18); 26 (19,20); 27 (21,22); 28 (23,24); 29 (25,26); 84 (12); 85 (14); 243 (a).

James Wilson: 176 (4); 177 (6,7); 181 (13).

Index

Bold page numbers refer to projects included in Selected and Current Works

Administrative and Student Services Building, City University of New York, Bronx, New York **136**, 246

Advanced Business Institute, IBM Corporation, Palisades, New York **30**, 243

Anchorage Historical and Fine Arts Museum, Anchorage, Alaska **18**, 243

Burke Library Renovation, Union Theological Seminary, New York, New York 242

Center West, Office/Retail/Parking, Los Angeles, California **166**, 243

Ceramics Corridor Innovation Center, Alfred, New York **112**, 244

Ceramics Corridor Innovation Center, Corning, New York **108**, 244

Columbus Center, Coral Gables, Florida **186**, 244

Davenport Downtown Plan and River Center Plaza, Davenport, Iowa **214**, 243

Dayton Residence, Wayzata, Minnesota 241

Elementary School, Aviano, Italy 242

Fine and Performing Arts Center, Pensacola, Florida **54**, 244

George M. Low Center for Industrial Innovation, Troy, New York **78**, 243

Hampton Roads History Center, Hampton, Virginia **44**, 244

Harlem International Trade Center, Harlem, New York **72**, 246

Health Services Building, College of Health Sciences, Massachusetts Institute of Technology, Cambridge, Massachusetts 242

Hudson View East Residential Development, Battery Park City, New York, New York **210**, 243

Intertech Corporation, Office Development Master Plan, Louden, Virginia **216**, 244

Laboratory Science Building, College of Staten Island, City University of New York, Staten Island, New York **124**, 245

Life Sciences Building, Ciba Pharmaceuticals, Summit, New Jersey **98**, 245

Metcalfe Student Center, Long Island University, Brooklyn, New York **128**, 246

Mission Park Residential Houses, Williamstown, Massachusetts 241

New Parliament House, Canberra, Australia 241

Newman Residence, Bedford, New York 241

Office and Assembly Building, Chesapeake, Virginia 241

Onondaga County Convention Center, Syracuse, New York **60**, 244

Outpatient Care Center, University of California at Los Angeles, California **86**, 244

PS 56, Richmond Elementary School, Staten Island, New York **140**, 246

PS 88, The Seneca School, Queens, New York **138**, 246

Revelle College Sciences Building, University of California at San Diego, LaJolla, California **92**, 245

Saint Joseph's College Comprehensive Plan, Patchogue, New York **218**, 245

Sherman Fairchild Center for the Life Sciences, Columbia University, New York, New York 241

Solana Office/Parking Complex, IBM Corporation and Maguire Thomas Partners, Westlake/Southlake, Texas **174**, 243

Southampton College Master Plan, Long Island University, Southampton, New York **220**, 245

Stafford Hall, Microbiology/Orthopaedics Research Building, University of Vermont, Burlington, Vermont **116**, 245

Student Housing, San Pietro al Natisone, Italy 242

Technical High School, Maniago, Italy 242

The Belvedere, Battery Park City, New York, New York **222**, 245

The Lighthouse Inc. Headquarters, New York, New York **196**, 245

300 Atlantic Street Office Building, Stamford, Connecticut **160**, 244

US Capitol Grounds Master Plan, Washington, DC 242

Virginia Air and Space Center/Hampton Roads History Center, Hampton, Virginia **44**, 244

Volvo Corporate Headquarters, Gothenburg, Sweden **146**, 243

Wainwright State Office Complex, St Louis, Missouri 242

Westlake Park Master Plan, IBM Corporation and Maguire Thomas Partners, Westlake, Texas 242

Zeckendorf Health Sciences Center, Long Island University, Brooklyn, New York **130**, 246